Present Day English
for Foreign Students

BOOK ONE

Ask the publishers for details of:

PRESENT DAY ENGLISH FOR FOREIGN STUDENTS
 Students' Books 1–3
 Teacher's Books 1–3
 Keys to the Exercises 1–3
PRESENT DAY ENGLISH READERS
 Graded supplementary readers, stages A–E
PRESENT DAY ENGLISH GRAMOPHONE RECORDS
PRESENT DAY ENGLISH LANGUAGE LABORATORY
 EXERCISES
PRESENT DAY ENGLISH WORK BOOKS
and other titles in the PRESENT DAY ENGLISH *series*

Present Day English
for Foreign Students

E. Frank Candlin, B.A. (Hons.)

*Formerly Principal of the Oxford College of Further
Education, Formerly Head of the Department
of English and Liberal Studies, University of
Wales Institute of Technology*

BOOK 1

HODDER AND STOUGHTON
LONDON SYDNEY AUCKLAND TORONTO

ISBN 0 340 09015 4

First published 1961

Fourth edition copyright © 1968 E. Frank Candlin
Fifteenth impression 1979
Illustrations copyright © 1961 Hodder & Stoughton Ltd

Illustrations by Bill Burnard

Printed in Great Britain for
Hodder and Stoughton Educational,
a division of Hodder and Stoughton Ltd,
Mill Road, Dunton Green, Sevenoaks, Kent
by Hazell Watson & Viney Ltd,
Aylesbury, Bucks

CONTENTS

6 CONTENTS

PREFACE

THIS Course is designed for teachers who are looking for a class-book which will ease their task of lesson-planning and at the same time enable their students to make rapid progress in understanding, speaking, reading and writing everyday English.

Each Lesson in Book One begins with a reading passage dealing with the daily life of an ordinary middle-class English family. A piece of conversation follows, so that similar material is treated colloquially and more formally in the same Lesson. Next come sentence-pattern drills illustrating structures and usage, arranged to a carefully graded scheme. The Lesson ends with a list of new words and idioms and a plentiful supply of exercises based on the material of that and earlier Lessons. Since most of the work in the initial stages of language learning must be oral, teachers will probably wish to spend a number of class periods on the material of Lessons 1 and 2, supplementing it from the classroom situation, before moving on to Lesson 3.

The controlled vocabulary—about 700 words in Book One, only about 50 of which are not in the *General Service Word List*—is given at the end. There is an easy reference index to the exercises and a list of the sentence patterns giving the teaching point covered and an example of each. To assist the teacher who wishes to make his own decisions on the teaching of grammar, the points illustrated by the sentence patterns are collected into two Grammar Summaries after Lessons 11 and 24. Throughout the book nothing is taken for granted except what has been covered in earlier Lessons. Phonetic transcripts are given for all new words and idioms as they occur, and again in the general vocabulary.

The pictures form an integral part of the book; they cover the vocabulary of the Lessons, and are intended to be used as the basis for classwork exercises. In the second half of the book a short anecdote in lighter vein has been added at the end of each Lesson.

Teaching English as a second language is a highly skilled art, particularly when rapid results are looked for. It is hoped that this Course, based on long practical experience, will make the task easier for the teacher and more enjoyable for the student.

E. F. C.

KEY TO PHONETIC SYMBOLS

Vowels and Diphthongs

iː	siː	see, sea	θin		thin
i	siks	six	ðiːz		these
e	ten	ten	sed		said
a	bad	bad	pak		pack
aː	haːd	hard	faːst		fast
o	hot	hot	wot		what
oː	doː	door	koːt		caught
u	tuk	took	put		put
uː	buːt	boot	juː		you
ʌ	sʌn	son, sun	kʌt		cut
əː	səː	sir	fəːst		first
ə	ˈmʌðə	mother	ˈsistə		sister
ei	keim	came	eit		eight
ou	ʃou	show	nou		no, know
ai	lait	light	main		mine
au	kau	cow	raund		round
oi	toi	toy	boi		boy
iə	niə	near	hiə		here, hear
eə	peə	pear, pair	weə		where
uə	ʃuə	sure	juə		you're

Consonants

t	teik	take	put		put
d	dog	dog	had		had
p	pen	pen	map		map
b	buk	book	ˈteibl		table
k	ˈkofi	coffee	buk		book
g	gou	go	dog		dog

f	fɔː	four	haːf	half
v	ˈveri	very	hav	have
m	ˈmʌðə	mother	kʌm	come
n	nain	nine	hand	hand
ŋ	siŋ	sing	ˈrʌniŋ	running
l	luk	look	dol	doll
θ	θin	thin	sauθ	south
ð	ðis	this	ˈfaːðə	father
s	siks	six	buks	books
z	rouz	rose	dogz	dogs
ʃ	ʃal	shall	fiʃ	fish
ʒ	ˈpleʒə	pleasure	ˈviʒn	vision
tʃ	matʃ	match	ˈkwestʃn	question
dʒ	bridʒ	bridge	peidʒ	page
r	rʌn	run	təˈmorou	tomorrow
w	wɔːl	wall	wen	when
j	jiə	year	jes	yes
h	hand	hand	hot	hot

LESSON 1

John and Mary Brown

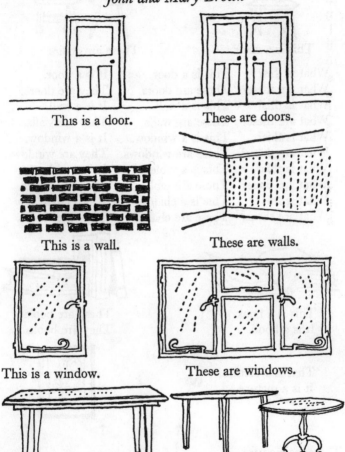

This is a door.

These are doors.

This is a wall.

These are walls.

This is a window.

These are windows.

This is a table.

These are tables.

This is a chair.

These are chairs.

What is this?	This is a door.	It is a door.
What are these?	These are doors.	They are doors.
What is this?	This is a wall.	It is a wall.
What are these?	These are walls.	They are walls.
What is this?	This is a window.	It is a window.
What are these?	These are windows.	They are windows.
What is this?	This is a table.	It is a table.
What are these?	These are tables.	They are tables.
What is this?	This is a chair.	It is a chair.
What are these?	These are chairs.	They are chairs.

This is a book.
It is a book.

These are books.
They are books.

That is a picture.
It is a picture.

Those are pictures.
They are pictures.

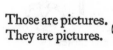

This is a cigarette.
It is a cigarette.

These are cigarettes.
They are cigarettes.

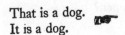

That is a dog.
It is a dog.

Those are dogs.
They are dogs.

This is a man.
This is John Brown.
John Brown is a man.
He is a man.

This is a woman.
This is Mary Brown.
Mary Brown is a woman.
She is a woman.

CONVERSATION

JOHN: I am a man. You are a woman.

MARY: I am Mary Brown. You are John Brown.

JOHN: This is a book. That is a pen.

MARY: What is this?

JOHN: That is a pen. What is this?

MARY: That is a book.

JOHN: Is this a book?

MARY: Yes, that is a book. Is this a pen?

JOHN: Yes, that is a pen.

MARY: Is this a door?

JOHN: No, that is not a door. It is (it's) a pen. Is this a window?

MARY: No, that is not a window. It's a book.

JOHN: Are these chairs?

MARY: Yes, those are chairs, and these are tables.

JOHN: Mary, what are these?

MARY: Those are books, John.

JOHN: Am I a man, Mary?

MARY: Yes, John, you are a man, and I am a woman.

SENTENCE PATTERNS

I.

This is a door.	These are doors.
This is a wall.	These are walls.
This is a window.	These are windows.
This is a table.	These are tables.
That is a chair.	Those are chairs.
That is a book.	Those are books.
That is a picture.	Those are pictures.
That is a dog.	Those are dogs.

2.

What is this?	This is a book.
What is this?	This is a pen.
What is that?	That is a dog.
What is that?	That is a window.
What are these?	These are books.
What are these?	These are pens.
What are those?	Those are dogs.
What are those?	Those are windows.

3.

It is a cigarette.	They are cigarettes.
It is a window.	They are windows.
It is a book.	They are books.
It is a wall.	They are walls.

John Brown is a man.
He is a man.
Mary Brown is a woman.
She is a woman.

I am a man.	I am John Brown.
I am a woman.	I am Mary Brown.

4.

Is this a man?	Yes, this is a man.
Is this a woman?	Yes, this is a woman.
Is that a dog?	Yes, that is a dog.
Is that a door?	Yes, that is a door.
Are these chairs?	Yes, these are chairs.
Are these tables?	Yes, these are tables.
Are those walls?	Yes, those are walls.
Are those pictures?	Yes, those are pictures.
Is this a book?	No, this is not (isn't) a book; it is (it's) a pen.
Is that a door?	No, that isn't a door; it's a window.

| Are these pens? | No, these are not (aren't) pens; they are pictures. |
| Are those tables? | No, they are not (aren't) tables; they are walls. |

5.

Am I a man?	Yes, you are a man.	Yes, you are.
Am I a woman?	Yes, you are a woman.	Yes, you are.
Are you a man?	Yes, I am a man.	Yes, I am.
Are you a woman?	Yes, I am a woman.	Yes, I am.
Is he a man?	Yes, he is a man.	Yes, he is.
Is she a woman?	Yes, she is a woman.	Yes, she is.
Mary, are you a man?	No, I am not a man.	No, I am not.
John, are you a woman?	No, I am not a woman.	No, I am not.
Is John a woman?	No, he is not a woman.	No, he is not.
Is Mary a man?	No, she is not a man.	No, she is not.

NEW WORDS

book (buk)
chair (tʃeə)
cigarette ('sigə'ret)
dog (dog)
door (doɪ)
man (man)
pen (pen)
picture ('piktʃə)
table ('teibl)
wall (woɪl)
window ('windou)
woman ('wumən)

John Brown ('dʒon 'braun)

Mary Brown ('meəri 'braun)

am (am, əm)
are (aɪ, ə)
is (iz)

a (ei, ə)
and (and, ənd, nd)
he (hiɪ, hi)
I (ai)
it (it)
no (nou)
not (not)
she (ʃiɪ, ʃi)

that (ðat)   those (ðouz)
these (ðiːz)   what (wot)
they (ðei)   yes (jes)
this (ðis)   you (juː, ju)

EXERCISES

Dictation

John Brown is a man. Mary Brown is a woman. This is John and that is Mary. This is a table and that is a chair. These are windows and those are walls. Is that a window? No, that is not a window; it is a door.

LESSON 2

In the Sitting Room

This is a man. He is John Brown; he is Mr Brown. He is in his sitting-room.

This is a woman. She is Mary Brown; she is Mrs Brown. She is in the sitting-room.

The man is Mr Brown; the woman is Mrs Brown. Mr and Mrs Brown are in the sitting-room; they are in the sitting-room.

Mr Brown has a book. The book is in his hand; he has a book in his hand. Mr Brown has a cigarette. The cigarette is in his mouth; he has a cigarette in his mouth.

Mrs Brown has a pen. The pen is in her hand; she has a pen in her hand. Mrs Brown has a bag. The bag is on the table; it is on the table.

Mr and Mrs Brown have a dog; they have a dog. The dog is in the room; it is in the room. The dog is under the table; it is under the table.

The pictures are on the walls; they are on the walls. The table is under the picture; it is under the picture. The dog is not under the chair; it is under the table. The pictures are not on the table; they are on the wall.

Mrs Brown hasn't a cigarette in her mouth; she has a pen in her hand. Mr Brown hasn't a pen in his hand.

CONVERSATION

JOHN: I am John Brown.

MARY: I am Mary Brown.

JOHN: I have a book. This is my book.

MARY: I have a pen; this is my pen.

JOHN: Have we a house?

MARY: Yes, we have a house; we are in our house. Have we a sitting-room?

JOHN: Yes, we have a sitting-room; this is our sitting-room. We are in our sitting-room.

MARY: Have you a book?

JOHN: Yes, I have a book; this is my book. It is in my hand. Have you a bag?

MARY: Yes, I have a bag. That is my bag; it is on the table. Have we a dog?

JOHN: Yes, we have a dog; it is under the table. What have you in your hand?

MARY: I have a pen in my hand. What have you in your mouth?

JOHN: I have a cigarette in my mouth. Where is the dog?
MARY: The dog is under the table. Where is your book?
JOHN: It is in my hand. Where are the pictures?
MARY: The pictures are on the wall.
JOHN: Have you a cigarette?
MARY: No, I haven't a cigarette. Is this your pen?
JOHN: No, that isn't my pen; it's your pen. My pen is on the
table.
MARY: No, it isn't. It's on the chair.

SENTENCE PATTERNS

6.

John has a book.
Mr Brown has a book.
He has a book.
The man has a book.
Mary has a pen.
Mrs Brown has a pen.
She has a pen.
The woman has a pen.
The room has a door.
It has a door.
I have a book.
I have a pen.
You have a bag.
You have a cigarette.
We have a house.
We have a dog.
They have a house.
They have a dog.
Mr and Mrs Brown have a house.

7.

Has the man a book?	Yes, he has a book.	Yes, he has.
Has he a book?	No, he has not (hasn't) a book.	No, he hasn't.
Has the woman a pen?	Yes, she has a pen.	Yes, she has.
Has she a pen?	No, she hasn't a pen.	No, she hasn't.
Has the room a door?	Yes, it has a door.	Yes, it has.
Has it a door?	No, it hasn't a door.	No, it hasn't.
Have I a book?	Yes, you have a book.	Yes, you have.
	No, you have not (haven't) a book.	No, you haven't.
Have we a dog?	Yes, we have a dog.	Yes, we have.
	No, we haven't a dog.	No, we haven't.
Have Mr and Mrs Brown a house?	Yes, they have a house.	Yes, they have.
Have they a house?	No, they haven't a house.	No, they haven't.

8.

Where am I?	You are in the room.
Where is Mr Brown?	He is in the house.
Where is Mrs Brown?	She is in the sitting-room.
Where is the dog?	It is under the table.
Where are we?	We are in the sitting-room.
Where are Mr and Mrs Brown?	They are in the sitting-room.
Where are the pictures?	They are on the walls.
Where are the books?	They are on the table.

9.

What have I in my hand?	You have a pen in your hand.	A pen.
What has he in his hand?	He has a book in his hand.	A book.
What has she in her hand?	She has a pen in her hand.	A pen.

What have you in your hand?	I have a pen in my hand.	A pen.
What have we on the table?	We have a book on the table.	A book.
What have they in the room?	They have a dog in the room.	A dog.

NEW WORDS

bag (bag)	have (hav, həv)
hand (hand)	
house (haus)	her (həɪ, hə)
mouth (mauθ)	his (hiz)
question ('kwestʃn)	in (in)
room (rum)	my (mai)
sitting-room ('sitiŋrum)	on (on)
	our (auə)
	the (ðə, ði, ðiɪ)
Mr ('mistə)	under ('ʌndə)
Mrs ('misiz)	we (wiɪ)
	where (weə)
has (haz, həz)	your (jɔɪ, juə)

EXERCISES

A. *Dictation*

Mr and Mrs Brown are in the sitting-room. Mr Brown is in a chair. He has a book in his hand and a cigarette in his mouth. Mrs Brown has a pen in her hand. Her bag is on the table. They have a dog; it is under the table. Mr and Mrs Brown have a house; this room is in the house.

B. *Questions*

Has Mr Brown a book in his hand? Yes, he has a book in his hand. Yes, he has.

1. Has Mrs Brown a pen in her hand?
2. What has Mr Brown in his hand?
3. What is on the wall?

4. What is on the table?
5. Where is the dog?
6. Is the dog in the room?
7. Where is the room?
8. Have Mr and Mrs Brown a house?
9. Where are the pictures?
10. Where is the bag?
11. Where is the sitting-room?
12. Has Mrs Brown a cigarette in her mouth?
13. Has Mr Brown a pen in his hand?
14. Is the dog on the table?
15. Is the bag on the table?
16. Is Mrs Brown in the chair?

C. The picture is on the . . . (*wall*)

1. Mr Brown is a . . .
2. Mr and Mrs Brown are in the . . .
3. Mr Brown has a . . . in his . . .
4. Mrs Brown is a . . .
5. Mrs Brown has a . . . in her . . .
6. The . . . is under the . . .
7. Mrs Brown hasn't a . . . in her . . .
8. The bag is on the . . .
9. Mr and Mrs Brown have a . . . It is under the . . .
10. Where are the pictures? . . . are on the . . .

LESSON 3

The Browns at Breakfast

MR AND MRS BROWN are in the dining-room. It is the dining-room of their house. Mr and Mrs Brown have a son and a daughter. David is their son; he is a boy. Susan is their daughter; she is a girl. David is tall. Susan is his sister. Susan is not tall; she is pretty. David is her brother.

Mrs Brown is sitting on a chair. Mr Brown is standing near the fire. David and Susan are sitting on chairs. David and Susan are eating their breakfast. They are eating bacon and eggs. David has a cup, a saucer, a plate, a knife, a fork and a spoon. They have bread, butter and marmalade on the table. Mr Brown is not sitting; he is standing near the fire.

He is not eating his breakfast; he is not hungry. Mrs Brown is not eating her breakfast; she is reading a letter. The letter is in her hand. A dog is on the carpet near the table. It is their dog; its name is Toby. The dog is not big. It is little. Cups and saucers, plates and spoons are on the table.

The Browns are having their breakfast. Mr and Mrs Brown are the father and mother; David and Susan are their son and daughter. Toby is their dog. Susan is speaking to David. David is not speaking to Susan; he is eating his breakfast. They are not eating their breakfast in the sitting-room; they are eating it in the dining-room. Mr Brown hasn't a letter. Susan and David haven't a letter.

CONVERSATION

MR BROWN: What have you in your hand, Mary?

MRS BROWN: It's a letter. I'm reading it.

MR BROWN: Are you eating your breakfast, Susan?

SUSAN: No, I'm speaking to David.

MRS BROWN: Are you eating your breakfast, David?

DAVID: Yes, Mother. Where is the dog?

SUSAN: The dog is there; he's on the carpet.

MRS BROWN: You're not eating your breakfast, John.

MR BROWN: No, I'm not hungry now.

SUSAN: I haven't a spoon, Mother.

MRS BROWN: Your spoon is there. It's on the table near your plate.

SUSAN: Yes, Mother. My spoon is here now.

DAVID: You're not eating your breakfast, Father.

MR BROWN: No, I'm not hungry, my boy.

MRS BROWN: David, have you a cup?

DAVID: Yes, I have. My cup is on the table.

MRS BROWN: What have you in your cup?

DAVID: I have coffee in my cup.

MRS BROWN: Susan, is this your cup near my plate?

SUSAN: No, Mother, it's not. My cup is here; it's near my
plate.

MRS BROWN: David, your Father isn't hungry. He's standing
near the fire.

DAVID: I'm hungry. I'm sitting at the table. I'm eating my
breakfast.

MR BROWN: What are you doing, Susan?

SUSAN: I'm drinking coffee. What are you doing, David?

DAVID: I'm eating my breakfast. What are you doing,
Mother?

MRS BROWN: I'm reading a letter.

SENTENCE PATTERNS

10.

Mr Brown is hungry.
Mr Brown is not hungry.   He isn't hungry.

Susan is pretty.
Susan is not pretty.   She isn't pretty.

David is tall.
David is not tall.   He isn't tall.

The dog is big.
The dog is not big.   It isn't big.

The dog is little.
The dog is not little.   It isn't little.

11.

Mr Brown is standing near the fire.
Mrs Brown is sitting on a chair.
The dog is sitting on the carpet.
David is eating his breakfast.

Susan is eating her breakfast.
Mrs Brown is reading a letter.
Susan is speaking to David.

12.

Mr Brown is not (isn't) eating his breakfast.
Mrs Brown is not (isn't) standing near the fire.
The dog isn't sitting on a chair.
Susan and David are not (aren't) standing.
Mr and Mrs Brown are not (aren't) speaking to David.

13.

Is David eating his breakfast?	Yes, he is.
Is Mr Brown standing near the fire?	Yes, he is.
Is Mr Brown reading a book?	No, he isn't.
Is David standing near the fire?	No, he isn't.
Is Susan speaking to David?	Yes, she is.
Are David and Susan sitting at the table?	Yes, they are.
Are Mr and Mrs Brown eating their breakfast?	No, they aren't.

NEW WORDS

bacon ('beikən)
boy (boi)
breakfast ('brekfəst)
bread (bred)
brother ('brʌðə)
butter ('bʌtə)
carpet ('kaːpit)
coffee ('kofi)
cup (kʌp)
daughter ('doːtə)
dining-room ('daininŋrum)
egg (eg)

father ('faːðə)
fire ('faiə)
fork (foːk)
girl (gəːl)
knife (naif)
letter ('letə)
marmalade ('maːməleid)
mother ('mʌðə)
plate (pleit)
saucer ('soːsə)
sister ('sistə)
son (sʌn)

spoon (spuːn)

David ('deivid)
Susan ('suːzən)

do (duː, du, də, d)
drink (driŋk)
eat (iːt)
read (riːd)
sit (sit)
speak (spiːk)
stand (stand)

at (at)
big (big)
here (hiə)
hungry ('hʌŋgri)
its (its)
little ('litl)
near (niə)
now (nau)
pretty ('priti)
tall (toːl)
their (ðeə)
there (ðeə)
to (tuː, tu, tə)

EXERCISES

A. *Dictation*

Mr and Mrs Brown are in their dining-room. Mr Brown is standing near the fire; he isn't hungry. Mrs Brown is reading a letter. Their son David and their daughter Susan are eating their breakfast. They have a little dog; it is under the table. David has a spoon in his hand. Susan hasn't a spoon in her hand; it is on the table near her plate. Susan is speaking to her brother.

B. *Questions*

1. Where are Mr and Mrs Brown?
2. Where is Mr Brown standing?
3. What is Mrs Brown reading?
4. What has David in his cup?
5. Where is Mrs Brown sitting?
6. What is David doing?
7. Where is the dog?
8. Where are the Browns eating their breakfast?
9. What is the dog doing?
10. Is Mr Brown hungry?
11. Is Susan reading a letter?

12. What is Susan doing?
13. Has Mrs Brown a pen in her hand?
14. What are David and Susan eating?
15. Are the Browns eating their breakfast in the sitting-room?

C. Mr and Mrs Brown are in the . . . (*dining-room*)
 1. The Browns are eating their . . .
 2. Mr Brown is . . . near the . . .
 3. Mrs Brown is . . . a . . .
 4. Susan is . . . to David.
 5. The dog is on the . . . near the . . .
 6. Mr Brown is not . . .
 7. Mr and Mrs Brown have a . . . and a . . .
 8. David and Susan are eating . . . and . . .
 9. Is David . . . his breakfast?

LESSON 4

Saying Good-bye

THIS is Mr Brown's car. Mr Brown is sitting in his car. Mrs Brown is standing near the gate. She is waving her hand; she is saying good-bye to Mr Brown. David is putting a bag into the car; it is Mr Brown's bag. David has not a hat on his head; his hat is in the house. The postman is giving a letter to Susan; she is saying "Thank you" to the postman. Susan's hat and coat are in the house.

Mr Brown's car is big; it is a big car. David is tall; he is a tall boy. Susan is pretty; she is a pretty girl. Mrs Brown is Mr Brown's wife; Mr Brown is Mrs Brown's husband. David is Mr Brown's son; Susan is Mr Brown's daughter. Susan's mother is Mrs Brown; Susan's father is Mr Brown. David is

Susan's brother; David's sister is Susan. Susan and David are saying good-bye to their father. Their dog is not there; he is in the house. The dog's name is Toby.

CONVERSATION

Mrs Brown: Have you your hat and coat, John?

Mr Brown: Yes, thank you, Mary. I haven't my bag; where is it, please?

Mrs Brown: David has it.

Mr Brown: Where's David? What's he doing?

Mrs Brown: He's putting your bag into the car.

Mr Brown: Are you taking a letter from the postman, Susan? Is it my letter, please?

Susan: No, Father, it isn't your letter. It's my letter. It's from Tom Smith.

Mrs Brown: Are you cold, John?

Mr Brown: No, thank you. I've my coat and hat and gloves. The car's warm.

Susan: Where's the dog? Where's Toby?

David: He's in the house.

Mr Brown: Good-bye, Mary. Good-bye, Susan. Good-bye, David.

Mrs Brown: Good-bye, John.

Susan: ⎫
David: ⎬ Good-bye, Father.

Susan: Where's Father going, Mother?

Mrs Brown: He's going to the station, Susan.

SENTENCE PATTERNS

14.

This is Mr Brown's car.
These are Mr Brown's gloves.

That is Mr Brown's house.
Those are Mr Brown's books.
This is Mrs Brown's coat.
These are Susan's letters.
That is David's hat.
Those are Mrs Brown's spoons.
Tom's letter is here.
David's hat is there.
Where is Mrs Brown's pen?
David is Susan's brother.
Mr Brown is David's father.

15.

Susan is pretty.	She is (she's) a pretty girl.
David is tall.	He is (he's) a tall boy.
The dog is hungry.	It is (it's) a hungry dog.
The house is big.	It is (it's) a big house.
The room is cold.	It is (it's) a cold room.
The coat is warm.	It is (it's) a warm coat.
This table is little.	This is a little table.
That girl is pretty.	That is (that's) a pretty girl.
I have a big car.	My car is big.
David has a pretty sister.	His sister is pretty.

16.

Susan is taking a letter from the postman.
David is putting a bag into the car.
Mrs Brown is saying good-bye to her husband.
Mr Brown is puttting a book on the table.
David is putting a spoon near his plate.
The dog is eating its breakfast under the table.

17.

Who is Mr Brown?	(He is) Mrs Brown's husband.
Who is Mrs Brown?	(She is) Mr Brown's wife.

Who is Susan?	(She is) David's sister.
Who is David?	(He is) Susan's brother.
Who is sitting in the car?	Mr Brown (is sitting in the car).
Who is waving good-bye?	Mrs Brown (is waving good-bye).
Who has a letter in his hand?	The postman (has a letter . . .)
Who is David's father?	Mr Brown (is David's father).
Who is Susan's mother?	Mrs Brown (is Susan's mother).
Who is putting a bag into the car?	David (is putting . . .)

NEW WORDS

car (kaɪ)	Tom Smith ('tom 'smiθ)
coat (kout)	
gate (geit)	give (giv)
glove (glʌv)	go (gou)
hat (hat)	put (put)
head (hed)	say (sei)
husband ('hʌzbənd)	take (teik)
name (neim)	wave (weiv)
postman ('poustmən)	
station ('steiʃn)	cold (kould)
wife (waif)	from (from, frəm)
	into ('intu)
Toby ('toubi)	warm (woim)
	who (huɪ)

Idioms

good-bye (gud'bai)
please (pliːz)
thank you ('θankjuɪ)

EXERCISES

A. *Dictation*

Mr Brown is sitting in his car. His wife is saying good-bye. David is putting his father's bag into the car. Susan is taking a letter from the postman. It isn't her father's letter; it is *her* letter. David hasn't a hat; his hat is in the house. Mr Brown isn't cold; his car is warm and he has a warm coat. Their dog isn't there; he's under the table in the sitting-room.

B. *Questions*

1. What is Mr Brown doing?
2. What is Mrs Brown doing?
3. Where is David?
4. What is he doing?
5. What has Susan in her hand?
6. Where is their dog?
7. What has Mr Brown on his head?
8. Has David a hat on his head?
9. Who is taking a letter from the postman?
10. Who is Mr Brown's son?
11. Is Mr Brown's bag in the car?
12. Is Susan's letter in the postman's hand?
13. Who is Mr Brown's daughter?
14. Who is Susan's brother?

C. David is a . . . boy. (*tall*)

1. Susan is a . . . girl.
2. Mr Brown has a . . . car.
3. The Browns have a . . . dog.
4. Mr Brown is not eating his breakfast; he is not . . .
5. Mr Brown has his hat and coat. He isn't . . .; he is . . .
6. David isn't a . . . boy; he is a . . . boy.
7. Mrs Brown hasn't a coat. Is she . . .?
8. David is . . .; Susan is . . .
9. David is eating his breakfast; he is . . .

LESSON 5

In the Street

MR BROWN is driving his car. He is going to the station. Mr Brown was in his house; now he is in his car. The car was in the garage; now it is in the street. The car was in front of the house; now it is near the station. A policeman is standing in the street. He is putting up his hand; he is stopping the cars in the street. The boys and girls are walking across the street.

Yesterday Mr Brown was in London; today he is going to London again. Now he is going by car to the station. He is not going by bus. He is going from his house to the station by car. He is going down the street to the station.

Mr Brown is speaking to a man in the street. The man is Mr Brook, Mr Fred Brook. He is Mr Brown's friend; they are friends. Mr Brook has a hat and a coat; he hasn't a bag.

Mr Brook hasn't a car; he is walking to the station. He is on foot. Yesterday he was warm. He had a hat, but he hadn't a coat. Mr Brook is short and fat; Mr Brown is tall and thin. Yesterday Mr Brook was in Mr Brown's house. He was at Mr Brown's. He had a cup of coffee there.

Near the pillar-box in this picture is the postman. He was in front of Mr Brown's house; now he is taking letters from the pillar-box. Yesterday the postman hadn't a coat; today he has a coat.

CONVERSATION

Mr Brown: Hello, Fred. How are you? Where are you going?

Mr Brook: Very well, thank you. I'm going to the station.

Mr Brown: Are you going to London?

Mr Brook: Yes, I am. I was in London yesterday, and I'm going there again today.

Mr Brown: Are you coming in my car?

Mr Brook: Thank you. The bus is slow. Your car is fast.

Mr Brown: Good! The policeman isn't stopping the cars now. Have you a newspaper?

Mr Brook: No, John. I haven't a newspaper. My newspaper is on the table at home.

Mr Brown: That boy is selling newspapers. That man is buying a newspaper.

Mr Brook: How's your wife today?

Mr Brown: She's very well, thank you, Fred.

Mr Brook: That's good. And how are Susan and David?

Mr Brown: They're well. How's Mrs Brook?

Mr Brook: She's not well, John. She's in bed today.

Mr Brown: I'm sorry. Here's the station. A train is standing in the station. Is it our train?

Mr Brook: Yes, it is. Hurry up!

SENTENCE PATTERNS

18.

Yesterday Mr Brown was in London.
Mr Brown was in his house.
He was in his car.
Mrs Brown was in her sitting-room.
She was in a bus.
I was in Mr Brown's car.
Mr and Mrs Brook were in Mr Brown's car.
They were in the train.
You were in London yesterday.
Mr Brown was near the fire.
The dog was under the table.
We were in the sitting-room.
The book was on the table.
The boys and girls were in the room.
The little boy was in the car.

19.

Mr Brown was not (wasn't) in London yesterday.
She was not (wasn't) in the sitting-room.
I was not (wasn't) in front of the house.
You weren't in Mr Brown's car.
They weren't in the dining-room.
David and Susan weren't in their father's car.
The postman wasn't near the pillar-box.
Mr Brown wasn't hungry.
The dog wasn't in the street.
We weren't in the dining-room.

20.

Was David in Mr Brown's car yesterday?   Yes, he was.
Was Mr Brook in London?   No, he wasn't.
Was Susan in the dining-room?   Yes, she was.

Were you in my car?	No, I wasn't.
Were Mr and Mrs Brown in London?	Yes, they were.
Were they in the street?	Yes, they were.
Were the pictures on the walls?	Yes, they were.
Was the dog on the carpet?	Yes, it was.
Was the bag under the table?	No, it wasn't.
Were the Browns in their sitting-room?	No, they weren't.

21.

Yesterday Mr Brook had a newspaper.
Mr Brown had a fast car.
I had a pen and a book.
Mr and Mrs Brown had a table in their sitting-room.
They had a house and a car.

22.

Susan hadn't a chair.
David hadn't a book.
He hadn't a car.
Mr and Mrs Brown hadn't a house.
They hadn't a daughter.
I hadn't a friend.
You hadn't a book.

NEW WORDS

bed (bed)
bus (bʌs)
foot (fut)
friend (frend)
garage ('garaːʒ, 'garidʒ)
home (houm)
newspaper ('njuːspeipə)
pillar-box ('piləboks)

policeman (pə'liːsmən)
street (striːt)
train (trein)

Brook (bruk)
Fred (fred)
London ('lʌndən)

buy (bai)
come (kʌm)
drive (draiv)
had (had, həd, d)
sell (sel)
stop (stop)
walk (wɔːk)
was (wɔz, wəz)
were (wəɪ, wə)

across (ə'kros)
again (ə'gein, ə'gen)

but (bʌt, bət)
by (bai)
down (daun)
fast (faːst)
fat (fat)
good (gud)
short (ʃɔːt)
slow (slou)
sorry ('sori)
thin (θin)
up (ʌp)

Idioms

at home (ət 'houm)
at Mr Brown's (ət 'mistə 'braunz)
by bus (bai 'bʌs)
by car (bai 'kaː)
by train (bai 'trein)
good! (gud)
hello! (he'lou)
how are you? ('hau ai 'juː)
hurry up! ('hʌri 'ʌp)
in bed (in 'bed)
in front of (in 'frʌnt əv)
on foot (on 'fut)
very well ('veri 'wel)
very well, thank you (veri 'wel 'θaŋkjuː)

EXERCISES

A. *Dictation*

Mr Brown | is driving to the station | in his car. | It is a fast car. | The policeman | is stopping the cars | and the boys and girls | are walking across the street. | Mr Brown is speaking | to his friend, Fred Brook. | They are going to London | by train. |

| They haven't a newspaper; | Mr Brook's newspaper is on the table | in his house. | A boy near the car | is selling newspapers. | The postman is taking letters | from the pillar-box. |

B. *Questions*

1. Where is Mr Brown going?
2. Where is Mr Brown's car?
3. What is the policeman doing?
4. Where was Mr Brown yesterday?
5. Who is Mr Brook?
6. What is Mr Brook doing?
7. How is Mrs Brook today?
8. Who are Susan and David?
9. What is the postman doing?
10. What is the boy selling in the street?
11. Who was at Mr Brown's house yesterday?
12. Where is Mrs Brook now?
13. What are the boys and girls doing?

C. *Plurals*

1. He is in London.   They are in London.
2. He has a friend.   ....
3. She is David's sister.   ....
4. He is my brother.   ....
5. Where is her brother?   ....
6. I wasn't in London yesterday.   ....
7. What is she doing?   ....
8. Is he taking the book?   ....
9. Am I walking across the street?   ....
10. The boy is going to his house.   ....
11. Where is his dog?   ....

D. *Negatives*

1. I have a book.   I haven't a book.
2. He is walking across the street.   ....
3. They are eating their breakfast.   ....

4. She is a pretty girl. ....
5. They have a house in London. ....
6. We are going to the station. ....
7. This is a dining-room. ....
8. He is standing near the fire. ....
9. They are driving their cars in ....
   the street.
10. Yesterday he had a coat. ....
11. He has a bag in the car. ....

E. Mrs Brown is . . . the sitting-room. (*in*)
   1. Mrs Brown has a pen . . . her hand.
   2. The dog is . . . the table.
   3. The picture is . . . the wall.
   4. Mr Brown is standing . . . the fire.
   5. David is speaking . . . his sister.
   6. David is putting a bag . . . the car.
   7. Mr Brown has a hat . . . his head.
   8. Have you a letter . . . me?
   9. Susan is taking a letter . . . the postman.
   10. The boys are walking . . . the street.

LESSON 6

At the Station

JOHN BROWN and his friend Fred Brook are at the station.
They came to the station in Mr Brown's car. They left the
car in the station garage and went into the station. Now Mr
Brown is getting his ticket from the booking-office. Mr Brook
is buying some cigarettes. Yesterday the train was late; today it is standing in the station.

Some men and women are coming through the gate.

The man at the gate is taking their tickets. A porter is carrying some bags to the train. The woman with the porter is carrying a small bag in her hand. She came to the station by taxi; now she is walking to the train. She has a black coat and hat and white gloves. She is carrying an umbrella. Some men and women are standing on the platform near the train; they are talking and waving good-bye to their friends on the train. A porter is closing the doors.

Now Mr Brown and his friend are running through the gate to the train. The porter is opening the door. Now they are in the train and the porter is closing the door again. Good-bye, Mr Brown!

CONVERSATION

MR BROWN: A ticket to London, please.
BOOKING CLERK: Single or return, sir?
MR BROWN : Return, please.
BOOKING CLERK: Are you going today, sir?
MR BROWN: Yes.

• • • • •

MR BROOK: A packet of cigarettes, please.
GIRL (*selling cigarettes*): Large or small, sir?
MR BROOK: Large, please. And a box of matches.
GIRL: Here are your cigarettes and matches, sir.
MR BROOK: Thank you. Good morning.

• • • • •

PORTER: Are you going to London, madam?
WOMAN (*in the black coat*): Yes, I am.
PORTER: Your train is standing in the station, madam. Is this your luggage?
WOMAN: Yes. I'm going to my friend's house in London.

PORTER: Have you your ticket?

WOMAN: Yes, I've my ticket in my bag here.

PORTER: Good. The train is there by the platform. Through that gate, madam.

. . . . .

MR BROWN: Have you your cigarettes and some matches?

MR BROOK: Yes. Have you your ticket?

MR BROWN: Yes. And I've a newspaper.

MR BROOK: Good! My ticket's in my pocket.

MR BROWN: The porter's closing the doors. We're late. Hurry up!

SENTENCE PATTERNS

23. Simple Past Tense

The porter is walking to the train.
The porter walked to the train.

Susan is talking to her brother.
She talked to her brother.

Mrs Brown is closing the door.
She closed the door.

Susan is waving to her father.
She waved to her father.

The policeman is stopping the car.
He stopped the car.

The boys and girls are crossing the street.
They crossed the street.

The porter is carrying the bags to the train.
He carried the bags to the train.

David is opening the window.
He opened the window.

24.

Mr Brown is taking his bag to the car.
He took his bag to the car.

Mr Brook is going to London.
He went to London.

David is coming to the station.
He came to the station.

The woman is standing on the platform.
She stood on the platform.

Mr Brown is driving his car.
He drove his car.

Susan is buying a coat and hat.
She bought a coat and hat.

The boy is selling newspapers.
He sold newspapers.

The Browns are sitting in their dining-room.
They sat in their dining-room.

Susan is speaking to the postman.
She spoke to the postman.

Mr Brown is leaving his car in the garage.
He left his car in the garage.

Mr Brook is getting his ticket from the booking-office.
He got his ticket from the booking-office.

The men are running through the gate.
They ran through the gate.

25.   *A—Some*

The porter is carrying a bag.
He is carrying some bags.

Mr Brook is buying a cigarette.
He is buying some cigarettes.

The man is taking a ticket.
He is taking some tickets.

Mr Brown has a match.
He has some matches.

The boy is selling a newspaper.
He is selling some newspapers.

Mr and Mrs Brown have a book.
They have some books.

I have a pen in my hand.
I have some pens in my hand.

Mrs Brown had an egg in her hand.
She had some eggs in her hand.

A boy is walking across the street.
Some boys are walking across the street.

A girl was in the room.
Some girls were in the room.

The policeman stopped a car.
The policeman stopped some cars.

NEW WORDS

booking-office ('bukiŋ ofis)
box (boks)
luggage ('lʌgidʒ)
madam ('madəm)
match (matʃ)
morning ('mɔːniŋ)
packet ('pakit)

platform ('platfɔːm)
pocket ('pokit)
porter ('pɔːtə)
sir (səː, sə)
taxi ('taksi)
ticket ('tikit)
umbrella (ʌm'brelə)

carry, carried ('kari, 'karid)
close, closed (klouz, klouzd)
cross, crossed (kros, krost)
get, got (get, got)
leave, left (liːv, left)
open, opened ('oupən,
  'oupənd)
run, ran (rʌn, ran)
talk, talked (tɔːk, tɔːkt)

an (an, ən)
black (blak)

large (laːdʒ)
late (leit)
or (ɔɪ)
of (ov, əv)
return (riˈtəɪn)
single ('siŋgl)
small (smɔːl)
some (sʌm)
through (θruː)
white (wait)
with (wið)

Idioms

good morning! (gudˈmɔɪniŋ)

EXERCISES

A. *Dictation*

In the station men and women are standing on the platform or walking to the trains. They came to the station by bus or by car or by taxi. Some men are buying cigarettes; a boy is selling newspapers. A porter is carrying some bags; a woman in a black coat is with the porter. A man is taking tickets at the gate. Mr Brown drove his car to the station and now he is buying a ticket at the booking-office; he is going to London. A train is standing in the station. Some men and women on the platform are saying good-bye to their friends in the train.

B. *Questions*

1. Where is Mr Brown getting his ticket?
2. Where are he and Mr Brook going?
3. What is Mr Brook buying from the girl?
4. What is the porter carrying?
5. What is the woman carrying in her hand?

6. What are the men and women on the platform doing?
7. Who is closing the doors of the train?
8. Where is the woman in the black coat going?
9. What is Mr Brown getting from the booking-office?
10. Where is the porter taking the bags?
11. Where is the train standing?
12. Who came to the station by taxi?
13. What has the porter in his hand?
14. Is a train standing in the station?

C. Mr Brown is . . . near the fire. (*standing*)

1. The porter is . . . the doors.
2. Mrs Brown is . . . a letter.
3. Susan is . . . her breakfast.
4. David is . . . a bag into the car.
5. Mr Brook is . . . to the station.
6. The boy is . . . newspapers.
7. Mr Brown is . . . a newspaper.
8. The porter is . . . a bag.
9. The boys and girls are . . . the street.
10. The policeman is . . . the cars.

D. *Plurals*

1. The woman is walking to the train.
2. The man is buying a newspaper.
3. He bought a packet of cigarettes.
4. The porter is closing the door.
5. The policeman stopped the car.
6. The boy is eating his breakfast.
7. He has a book in his hand.
8. A man is running through the gate.
9. She is putting a book on the table.

10. She is sitting in the dining-room with her friend.
11. I have a book in my hand.

E. *What are they doing in the picture?*

    1. Mr Brown. 2. Mr Brook. 3. The porter. 4. The booking-clerk. 5. The woman in the black coat. 6. The man at the gate. 7. The men and women on the platform. 8. The porter on the platform.

F. The bag is . . . the table. (*on*)
    1. The cup is . . . my plate.
    2. Susan is waving . . . her father.
    3. John Brown and his friend are . . . the station.
    4. They left the car . . . the station garage.
    5. He is getting his ticket . . . the booking-office.
    6. They are running . . . the gate.
    7. Mr Brown is walking . . . his friend.
    8. They are standing . . . the platform . . . the train.
    9. He is putting his ticket . . . his pocket.
    10. The policeman is putting . . . his hand.

LESSON 7

Taxi!

MR BROWN went to London by train with his friend Mr
Fred Brook. They got out at Victoria Station. Mr Brown was
late, so he took a taxi from the station to his office. He works
in a bank in London; he is the manager.

The taxi came round a corner near the Houses of Parliament and a car ran into it. A window broke and a wheel
came off. Mr Brown fell and hit his head on the door. The
car did not stop; it drove away. A policeman shouted, but the
car did not stop.

Mr Brown got out of the taxi. The policeman spoke to

Mr Brown and to the taxi-driver; he was very angry. He wrote the number of the car in his little black book; the number was XYZ 123. The taxi-driver was angry too; he shouted and waved his arms.

The policeman asked many questions. Then Mr Brown walked to his bank. There he sat on a chair and had a cup of tea. He did not work that morning.

CONVERSATION

MR BROOK: Here we are at Victoria.

MR BROWN: Yes. I'm late this morning. Good-bye, Fred. Taxi!

TAXI-DRIVER: Where to, sir?

MR BROWN: The Strand. London Bank. I'm late.

TAXI-DRIVER: All right, sir.

. . . . .

TAXI-DRIVER (*to Policeman*): He came round that corner and he ran into my taxi. He didn't stop.

POLICEMAN: Did you get his number?

TAXI-DRIVER: Yes, I got the number: XYZ 123.

POLICEMAN: Did you see the driver?

TAXI-DRIVER: Yes. He was a tall man with black hair. He had a blue coat, but he hadn't a hat.

MR BROWN: I'm late. My office is in the Strand. The London Bank. I'm the Manager.

POLICEMAN: What is your name, sir, please?

MR BROWN: Brown, John Brown.

POLICEMAN: Thank you, sir. Are you hurt?

MR BROWN: No. I only hit my head on the door of the taxi.

POLICEMAN: Did you see the number of the car, sir?

MR BROWN: No, I didn't.

POLICEMAN: Did you see the driver?

MR BROWN: No. He came round the corner and ran into the taxi. I didn't see his face.

POLICEMAN: All right, sir. You said the London Bank?

MR BROWN: Yes. In the Strand. I'm the manager.

POLICEMAN: Thank you, sir.

SENTENCE PATTERNS

26.   Simple Past Tense—Negative

Mr Brown walked to the office.
Mr Brown did not (didn't) walk to the office.

The policeman shouted to the driver.
The policeman did not (didn't) shout to the driver.

Mr Brook talked to the porter.
Mr Brook did not (didn't) talk to the porter.

The porter closed the door.
He did not (didn't) close the door.

The driver got the number.
The driver did not (didn't) get the number.

He came round the corner.
He did not (didn't) come round the corner.

Mr Brown took a taxi.
Mr Brown did not (didn't) take a taxi.

They went to the office.
They did not (didn't) go to the office.

The policeman stood near the taxi.
The policeman did not (didn't) stand near the taxi.

Mrs Brown drove to the station.
She did not (didn't) drive to the station.

Mr Brown saw the driver.
He did not (didn't) see the driver.

27. Simple Past Tense—Questions

Did the driver see the number?	Yes, he did.
	No, he didn't.
Did the car come round the corner?	Yes, it did.
	No, it didn't.
Did Mr Brown take a taxi?	Yes, he did.
	No, he didn't.
Did you go to the office, Mr Brown?	Yes, I did.
	No, I didn't.
Did Mrs Brown drive the car?	Yes, she did.
	No, she didn't.
Did Mr Brown and Mr Brook go to London?	Yes, they did.
	No, they didn't.
Did the driver close the door?	Yes, he did.
	No, he didn't.
Did the policeman speak to the driver?	Yes, he did.
	No, he didn't.
Did they walk to the station?	Yes, they did.
	No, they didn't.
Did the porters close the doors?	Yes, they did.
	No, they didn't.

NEW WORDS

arm (aɪm)
bank (baŋk)
corner ('kɔɪnə)
driver ('draɪvə)
face (feis)
hair (heə)
manager ('manidʒə)
number ('nʌmbə)
office ('ofis)
parliament ('paɪləmənt)
tea (tiɪ)
wheel (wiɪl)

Strand (strand)

Victoria Station (vik'tɔɪriə 'steiʃn)

ask, asked (aɪsk, aɪskt)
break, broke (breik, brouk)
fall, fell (fɔɪl, fel)
hit, hit (hit, hit)
see, saw (siɪ, sɔɪ)
shout, shouted (ʃaut, ʃautid)
work, worked (wɜɪk, wɜɪkt)
write, wrote (rait, rout)

all (ɔɪl)
angry ('aŋgri)
away (ə'wei)

blue (bluɪ)   out (aut)
hurt (həɪt)   right (rait)
many ('meni)   round (raund)
off (of)   so (sou)
only ('ounli)   too (tuɪ)

Idioms

all right! ('oɪl rait)
here we are ('hiə wi 'aɪ)
the number of the car (ðə 'nʌmbə əv ðə 'kaɪ)
they got out (ðei 'got 'aut)
to run into (tə 'rʌn 'intə)
where to? ('weə 'tuɪ)

EXERCISES

A. Questions

1. Where did Mr Brown get out of his train?
2. What did he take at the station?
3. What was the name of the station?
4. What came round a corner and hit the taxi?
5. Who shouted at the driver?
6. What was the number of the car?
7. Was Mr Brown hurt?
8. Where is Mr Brown working?
9. Where is Mr Brown's bank?
10. What did the policeman write in his little book?
11. Was the driver of the car tall or short?
12. What did Mr Brown have in his room at the bank?
13. Did Mr Brown see the driver's face?
14. Was a policeman standing in the street?

B. Did the policeman (SEE, *seeing*, *saw*) Mr Brown?

1. Did Mr Brown (*go, going, went*) to the office yesterday?
2. Susan is not (*sat, sitting, sit*) on the chair.
3. Did the driver (*shout, shouted, shouting*) at the policeman?
4. The porter is not (*walk, walked, walking*) through the gate.

5. Did Mr Brook (*come, came, coming*) to the office yesterday?
6. Mr Brown is (*drove, drive, driving*) his car.
7. Yesterday Mrs Brown (*is going, went*) to the town.
8. Is David (*go, going, went*) to London today?
9. Did the driver (*got, getting, get*) the number?
10. Is Susan (*speak, speaking, spoke*) to the postman?

C. Mr Brown *is going* to London.
   Mr Brown *went* to London.

1. David *is breaking* a window.
   David . . . a window.
2. The policeman *is shouting* to the driver.
   The policeman . . . to the driver.
3. Mrs Brown *is asking* a question.
   Mrs Brown . . . a question.
4. Susan *is taking* a book from the table.
   Susan . . . a book from the table.
5. The woman *is coming* to the station by taxi.
   The woman . . . to the station by taxi.
6. The porter *is standing* on the platform.
   The porter . . . on the platform.
7. David *is driving* his father's car.
   David . . . his father's car.
8. I *am buying* a newspaper.
   I . . . a newspaper.
9. The girl *is selling* a packet of cigarettes.
   The girl . . . a packet of cigarettes.
10. Mrs Brown *is sitting* in the car.
    Mrs Brown . . . in the car.

D. *Negatives*

Mr Brown *saw* his friend. Mr Brown *didn't see* his friend.

1. Mrs Brown is eating her breakfast.
2. They have a fast car.
3. David bought a box of matches.
4. Mr and Mrs Brown are in the dining-room.

5. This is Mr Brown's son David.
6. The policeman shouted to the driver.
7. The porter is closing the door.
8. You are late this morning, David.
9. The policeman and the driver were angry.
10. We were in London yesterday.
11. The boy hit the dog.
12. Susan wrote a letter to Tom.
13. The policeman asked a question.
14. Mr Brown saw his friend at the station.
15. The porter opened the door.

E. The policeman is stopping the cars. Is the policeman stopping the cars?

1. The taxi is coming round the corner.
2. The Browns spoke to their friends.
3. Mr Brook sat in Mr Brown's car.
4. Mr Brown took the picture from the wall.
5. Susan went to London yesterday.
6. David broke a window in the dining-room.
7. The postman stood in front of the house.
8. You have a letter in your hand, Susan.
9. Mrs Brown is waving good-bye to her husband.
10. The porter carried the bags to the train.

F. She is putting . . . her umbrella. (*up*)

1. He went to London . . . train.
2. He went . . . his friend, Mr Brook.
3. They got . . . the train . . . Victoria Station.
4. He took a taxi . . . the station . . . his office.
5. The taxi came . . . a corner.
6. The wheel came . . .
7. He hit his head . . . the door.
8. The car drove . . .
9. He wrote the number . . . his book.
10. The car ran . . . the taxi.

LESSON 8
In the Garden

THE Browns have a very nice garden round their house. It has some tall trees and many flowers. Mr and Mrs Brown work hard in their garden. Now Mrs Brown is in the garden getting some flowers. She will put the flowers in the dining-room and in the sitting-room.

Susan is sitting in a chair in the garden; she is reading a book. She took the book from the table in the house. Susan did not go to work today, so she is at home. David is saying good-bye to his mother. He is running through the gate;

he is going to school. He will go to school by bus. At school
he will work with his friends. He will have lunch at school.
Mrs Brown and Susan will have lunch at home. Mr Brown
went to London today; he is in London now and will have
his lunch there. This afternoon he will come to the station by
train, and he will drive from the station to his house by car.
Mrs Brown will be at home. Susan will be with her friend
Tom Smith in his car. They will go to the town this afternoon
and have tea there.

Now the dog is in the garden with Mrs Brown and Susan.
He was in the dining-room under the table; now he is standing near Susan's chair. He is putting his feet on the arm of
the chair. Susan will give him a chocolate; she has some chocolates in her pocket. She bought the chocolates in the town
yesterday. Toby, the dog, will take the chocolate in his
mouth and eat it quickly.

CONVERSATION

MRS BROWN: David, are you going to school now?

DAVID: Yes, Mother. I'll take the bus at the corner of the
street.

MRS BROWN: You're late. Hurry up! Run quickly.

DAVID: All right, Mother. Good-bye!

MRS BROWN: Good-bye! And work hard. What are you
doing, Susan?

SUSAN: I'm reading a book. It's very good. I took it from the
table in the sitting-room.

MRS BROWN: Where's Toby?

SUSAN: He's here, on the grass under my chair.

MRS BROWN: Get me a knife from the house, please, Susan.
I'll cut some flowers for the sitting-room and dining-
room.

SUSAN: All right, Mother.
Here you are. This knife was on the table.

MRS BROWN: Thank you. Now cut some flowers for the sitting-room, please, and I'll cut some for the dining-room. We'll have our lunch at home.

SUSAN: I shall go to town with Tom this afternoon. Is Father in London today?

MRS BROWN: Yes, he went by train this morning.

SUSAN: Did he take the car?

MRS BROWN: Yes, he drove to the station. He'll have his lunch in London and come home this afternoon.

SUSAN: Here are the flowers for the sitting-room, Mother.

MRS BROWN: Thank you. Those are nice. Put the yellow and white flowers in the sitting-room and these blue and red flowers in the dining-room, please.

SUSAN: Yes, Mother. Are you hungry? I am.

MRS BROWN: All right. We'll have lunch soon.

SUSAN: What is there for lunch?

MRS BROWN: I'll go and see.

SENTENCE PATTERNS

28. The Future Tense

David will go to school tomorrow.
He will have his lunch at school.
Mr Brown will be in London tomorrow.
Mrs Brown and Susan will have their lunch at home.
Susan will take the book from the table.
She will sit in a chair in the garden.
David will work with his friends in school.
They will come to the house by bus.
The dog will sit under the chair in the garden.
It will eat a chocolate.
Susan and Tom will drive to the town in his car.
Mr Brown will go to London by train tomorrow.
He will leave his car at the station.

29.   The Imperative

Go to school, David. You're late.
Put the flowers on the table, Susan.
Take the dog into the garden, John.
Open the door, please.
Close the window, please. I'm cold.
Read this book; it's very good.
Cross the road near the policeman, boys and girls.
Come here, David.
Get your ticket from the booking-office.
Leave your bag in the car and come into the house.
Carry your mother's bag, David.
Write a letter to the Bank Manager.
Do your work well, David.
Get in, and I'll drive you to the station.

30.   The Imperative—Negative

Don't put these flowers in the dining-room, Susan.
Don't put that book in the fire.
Don't go to school this morning, David.
Don't cross the road in front of a car.
Don't shut the door; a man is getting into the train.
Don't drive to town this afternoon; sit in the garden.
Don't carry that bag, Mother.
Don't leave your bag in the car.
Don't close the window, please.
Don't take the dog into the dining-room, John.
Don't go by bus; go by train.

NEW WORDS

afternoon ('aɪftə'nuɪn)   grass (graɪs)
chocolate ('tʃoklət)   lunch (lʌntʃ)
flower ('flauə)   school (skuɪl)
garden ('gaɪdn)   town (taun)

tree (triː)	him (him)
	me (miː)
answer, answered ('aːnsə, 'aːnsəd)	nice (nais)
	quickly ('kwikli)
cut, cut (kʌt, kʌt)	red (red)
will (wil)	soon (suːn)
	tomorrow (tə'morou)
for (foː, fə)	yellow ('jelou)
hard (haːd)	

Idioms

this afternoon (ðis' aːftə'nuːn)

Here you are ('hiə juː'aː)

EXERCISES

A. *Dictation*

Mrs Brown and her daughter Susan are in their garden. They have a nice garden with many flowers in it. Mrs Brown is getting some white and yellow flowers; she will put them in the sitting-room. Susan is sitting in a chair reading a book. David Brown will have his lunch in school today; Mrs Brown and Susan will have their lunch in the dining-room at home. Mr Brown and his friend Fred Brook are in London; they went there by train this morning. They will drive home from the station in Mr Brown's car this afternoon.

B. *Answer these questions:*

1. What is Mrs Brown doing in the garden?
2. Where is Susan?
3. Where is the dog standing?
4. Where is David going?
5. What did Susan buy in the town yesterday?
6. Where did Mr Brown go this morning?
7. Where is Mrs Brown's garden?
8. What is the dog eating?

9. Did Mr Brown take his car to the station today?
10. Is Mrs Brown sitting in a chair in the garden?
11. What is in Mrs Brown's garden?
12. Is Mr Brown's car in the garage today?

C. *Put the right word into these sentences:*

1. Susan (*is sitting, sat, will sit*) in the garden now.
2. Tomorrow Mr Brown and Mr Brook (*drove, are driving, will drive*) to the station.
3. Did Mrs Brown (*got, getting, get*) yellow flowers from the garden?
4. Is Mr Brown (*walk, walking, walked*) to the station?
5. Susan, (*taking, took, take*) these flowers into the house, please.
6. Mr Brook did not (*bought, buying, buy*) a newspaper at the station.
7. Is Susan (*sit, sat, sitting*) in the garden?
8. David (*will break, broke, is breaking*) a window yesterday.
9. Susan (*will give, gave, is giving*) some flowers to her mother tomorrow.
10. David is not (*went, going, go*) to school today.

D. *Give short answers to these questions:*

Is David going to school today? (*Yes, he is.*)

1. Are we in the garden?
2. Did they go to London yesterday?
3. Has Mrs Brown a nice garden?
4. Were Mr Brown and Mr Brook at the station this morning?
5. Are the boys and girls crossing the street?
6. Did she put the book on the table?
7. Have the Browns a table in their dining-room?
8. Am I sitting in the garden?
9. Did Susan put the flowers in the sitting-room?
10. Is the knife on the table in the dining-room?

E. *Put these sentences into the plural:*

The book is on the table. (*The books are on the table.*)

1. The girl is cutting a flower for her mother.
2. The boy broke a window in his house.
3. He will take a book to school tomorrow.
4. Has she a book in her hand?
5. He did not take the picture from the wall.
6. He is sitting in the garden of his house.
7. The woman is reading a letter from her friend.
8. This is my book and that is my pen.
9. Is he driving his car today?
10. He is not working in his office today.

F. They have a nice garden . . . their house. (*round*)

1. Susan is sitting . . . the garden.
2. David is running . . . the gate.
3. She took the book . . . the table.
4. David will work hard . . . school.
5. Mrs Brown and Susan will have lunch . . . home.
6. He went to the station . . . car.
7. The dog is . . . Susan's chair.
8. Mrs Brown is cutting some flowers . . . the sitting-room.
9. Susan is at home . . . her mother.
10. David is running . . . the road.

G. Mr Brown went to London yesterday. Did Mr Brown go to London yesterday?

1. Susan gave a chocolate to the dog.
2. Mrs Brown and Susan had their lunch at home.
3. The policeman answered your questions.
4. Mr Brown talked to the driver.
5. Tom drove to the station.

LESSON 9

The Browns at Dinner

THE Browns are having dinner in their dining-room; it is seven o'clock in the evening. Mr Brown went to London at nine o'clock this morning by train. He took his car to the station. He came back at about six o'clock this evening. He will not go to London tomorrow; he will stay at home. Tomorrow will be Saturday.

Mrs Brown stayed at home all day. In the morning she was in the garden with Susan. In the afternoon she worked in the house. She will not work hard tomorrow; tomorrow will be Saturday.

David went to school this morning. He had his lunch in school at one o'clock. In the afternoon he played football with his friends at school. He will not be in school tomorrow; tomorrow will be Saturday.

At breakfast this morning Mr Brown wasn't hungry; now he is hungry, and he's eating a good dinner. Mrs Brown is happy; her husband and children are at home and the dinner is good. There are flowers in every room in the house.

Tom Smith is having dinner with the Browns. Tom Smith is Susan's boy-friend. He is tall and good-looking. He is sitting near Susan at table. This afternoon he took Susan to town in his car, and they had tea there.

CONVERSATION

MRS BROWN: You aren't eating, Tom. Will you have some cheese?

TOM: No, thank you, Mrs Brown. The dinner was very good. You are a good cook.

MRS BROWN: Thank you, Tom. And you're a very nice boy!

MR BROWN: Some wine, Tom? Your glass is empty.

TOM: Thank you. A little, please.

MR BROWN: Where shall we go tomorrow?

SUSAN: To the sea.

DAVID: Yes, to the sea.

MR BROWN: Shall we take the car, or shall we go by train?

MRS BROWN: By car. Will you come, Tom?

TOM: Yes, thank you. I shan't work tomorrow, Saturday.

MRS BROWN: Did you see Fred Brook this morning, John?

MR BROWN: Yes, I saw him in the street near the station. We went to London by train.

MRS BROWN: How is his wife?

MR BROWN: She's not very well. She was in bed today.

MRS BROWN: I'm sorry. Is her daughter Mary in London now?

MR BROWN: No, she's in Birmingham. She'll come home now her mother isn't well.

MRS BROWN: Will you have some fruit, Tom?

TOM: Yes, thank you. A pear, please.

MRS BROWN: Did you play football this afternoon, David?

DAVID: Yes, Mother. We played this afternoon. It was a good game. I shan't play tomorrow; we'll go to the sea.

MRS BROWN: Shall we take the dog?

MR BROWN: Will he be good in the car?

SUSAN: Yes, he'll be good. It only takes an hour by car. You're a good dog, aren't you, Toby?

TOBY: Bow-wow!

MR BROWN: All right. We'll start at ten o'clock in the morning.

SENTENCE PATTERNS

31.　　　　　　　Future Tense—Questions

Will David go to school tomorrow?	Yes, he will. No, he won't.
Will Susan take the book from the table?	Yes, she will. No, she won't.
Will Mr Brown eat his dinner?	Yes, he will. No, he won't.
Will they go by car?	Yes, they will. No, they won't.
Will Tom be in London tomorrow?	Yes, he will. No, he won't.
Will Mr Brown eat his breakfast tomorrow?	Yes, he will. No, he won't.

32.

Future Tense—Negative

Mr Brown will not (won't) go to London tomorrow.
We shall not (shan't) take the dog to the sea.
David will not (won't) play football on Saturday.
I shall not (shan't) have my lunch at home.
The boys will not (won't) come home by car.
They won't work tomorrow.
He won't stay at home this afternoon.
I shan't give these flowers to my mother.
Mrs Brown won't sit in the garden this afternoon.

33.

Time—Hours

What time is it, please?

It is one o'clock.   1 A.M. or 1 P.M.*
It is two o'clock.   2 A.M. or 2 P.M.
It is three o'clock.   3 A.M. or 3 P.M.
It is four o'clock.   4 A.M. or 4 P.M.
It is five o'clock.   5 A.M. or 5 P.M.
It is six o'clock.   6 A.M. or 6 P.M.
It is seven o'clock.   7 A.M. or 7 P.M.
It is eight o'clock.   8 A.M. or 8 P.M.
It is nine o'clock.   9 A.M. or 9 P.M.
It is ten o'clock.   10 A.M. or 10 P.M.

* A.M. = *ante meridiem* (Latin), before noon.
P.M. = *post meridiem* (Latin), after noon.

It is eleven o'clock.	II A.M. or II P.M.
It is twelve o'clock.	12 noon or 12 midnight.
It is one o'clock in the morning.	(01.00)
It's six o'clock in the morning.	(06.00)
It's nine o'clock in the morning.	(09.00)
It's twelve o'clock midday.	(12.00)
It's three o'clock in the afternoon.	(15.00)
It's six o'clock in the evening.	(18.00)
It's nine o'clock in the evening.	(21.00)
It's eleven o'clock at night.	(23.00)
It's twelve o'clock midnight.	(24.00)

NEW WORDS

boy-friend ('boi 'frend)
cheese (tʃiːz)
children ('tʃildrən)
cook (kuk)
day (dei)
dinner ('dinə)
evening ('iːvniŋ)
football ('futbɔːl)
fruit (fruːt)
game (geim)
glass (glaːs)
hour (auə)
night (nait)
pear (peə)
sea (siː)
wine (wain)

Birmingham ('bəːmiŋəm)
Saturday ('satədi)

play, played (plei, pleid)
shall (ʃal, ʃəl)
start, started (staːt, staːtid)
stay, stayed (stei, steid)

about (ə'baut)
back (bak)
empty ('emti)
every ('evri)
good-looking ('gud 'lukiŋ)
happy ('hapi)
midday ('midei)
midnight ('midnait)
o'clock (ə'klok)
when (wen)

one (wʌn)
two (tuː)
three (θriː)
four (fɔː)
five (faiv)
six (siks)
seven ('sevn)
eight (eit)
nine (nain)
ten (ten)
eleven (i'levn)
twelve (twelv)

Idioms

all day (oɪl 'dei)
at table (ət 'teibl)
it's one o'clock (its 'wʌn ə'klok)
stay at home ('stei ət 'houm)
to come back (tə 'kʌm 'bak)
what time is it? ('wot 'taim iz it)

EXERCISES

A. *Dictation*

The Browns have a very nice house and garden. Now they are having dinner in the dining-room. Susan's boy-friend, Tom Smith, is sitting near Susan and he is eating a pear. It is a good dinner. In the dining-room they have some red and blue flowers; Mrs Brown put them there this afternoon. To-morrow will be Saturday, and the Browns and their friend will go to the sea. They will take Toby the dog. They won't go by train; they'll go by car.

B. *Answer these questions:*

1. Who is having dinner in the dining-room?
2. Will Tom Smith work on Saturday?
3. Where did Susan go this afternoon?
4. What will Mr Brown put in Tom's glass?
5. What fruit is Tom eating?
6. How is Mrs Brook today?
7. Where did Mr Brown meet his friend Fred Brook?
8. Who played football with David this afternoon?
9. Where is Mr Brook's daughter Mary?
10. Where will the Browns go on Saturday?
11. Where did Mrs Brown get the flowers?
12. What is there in Tom's glass?

C. *Answer these questions:*

1. What time did Mr Brown go to the station today?
2. When did he come home?

3. What time did the Browns have dinner?
4. What time did David have lunch at school?
5. What time will the Browns go to the sea on Saturday?
6. Is 8 P.M. in the afternoon or in the evening?
7. Is 10 A.M. in the morning or in the afternoon?
8. Is 3 P.M. in the morning, afternoon or evening?
9. Is 21.00 in the morning, afternoon or evening?
10. When is 18.00?
11. When is 09.00?
12. When is 24.00?

D. *Answer these questions with* "Yes, he is", "No, they aren't", *etc.:*

1. Is Mr Brown in London today?
2. Are the Browns having dinner in their dining-room?
3. Did Mr Brown meet Mr Brook this morning?
4. Did Mrs Brown go to town this morning?
5. Will the Browns go to the sea on Saturday?
6. Will Tom Smith work on Saturday?
7. Has Mr Brook a car?
8. Have the Browns a nice garden?
9. Is Mr Brown's house in London?
10. Have the Browns three children?

E. *Put these sentences into the negative:*

David *is going* to school today. David *isn't going* to school today.

1. The Browns *are having* dinner in the garden.
2. Susan *went* to London today.
3. Tom Smith *will work* on Saturday.
4. Mr Brook *has* a car.
5. The woman *is carrying* her bag to the train.
6. Mrs Brown *has* a flower in her hand.
7. Mr and Mrs Brown *went* to the sea today.
8. The policeman *wrote* in his little book.
9. The taxi-driver *shouted* to Mr Brown.
10. David *will play* football with his friends tomorrow.

F. *Put these sentences into the singular:*

These boys are playing football. This boy is playing football.

1. The books are on the tables.
2. The porters will close the doors.
3. They have some flowers in their hands.
4. Did they eat some pears?
5. The girls are eating some chocolates.
6. Some men are standing on the platform.
7. Did the women carry their bags to the train?
8. The girls are giving some letters to the postman.
9. The men are talking to their friends at the station.
10. They aren't putting the letters on the table.

G. David went to school yesterday. Did David go to school yesterday?

1. Susan stayed at home yesterday.
2. David played football this morning.
3. Mr Brown came home at six o'clock.
4. You saw him in the street yesterday.
5. David put the bag into the car.
6. Mr Brook drove to work this morning.
7. The taxi-driver saw the number of the car.
8. Susan took this book from the dining-room.
9. Mrs Brown waved to her husband.
10. The girl sold a box of matches to Mr Brown.

LESSON 10

At the Seaside

THE Browns live in Bishopton. Bishopton is a small town near London. Mr Brown works in London. He goes to London in the morning on Monday, Tuesday, Wednesday, Thursday and Friday; he goes to London every day except Saturday and Sunday. Mrs Brown, his wife, works in the house. David Brown, their son, goes to school every day except Saturday and Sunday. On Saturday the Browns often go in the car to the country or to the sea. David is seventeen years old and Susan is nineteen; her boy-friend, Tom Smith, is twenty. He sometimes works on Saturday.

Today they are all at the seaside. Mrs Brown is sitting in a deck-chair; she is reading a book. Mr Brown and David are playing cricket with a ball on the sand. Susan and Tom are swimming in the water. Soon they will have tea. Mrs Brown will get some tea from the little shop. The dog is asleep on the sand near Mrs Brown's chair. The sun is shining; the sea and the sky are blue.

Four children are running across the sand to the sea; they will swim in the water. One boy has a large ball; he is holding it in his two hands. Three boats are on the sea. In one boat a man is fishing.

In the evening the Browns will drive home in the car. They will be tired but happy; they all like a day by the sea.

CONVERSATION

MRS BROWN: Come here, everyone! Tea's ready.

MR BROWN: Good! I'm tired. A cup of tea, please.

SUSAN: The water's warm. I like the sea.

MRS BROWN: How far did you swim?

SUSAN: To the little boat, out there.

DAVID: Father and I played cricket. He's not very good.

MR BROWN: Yes, David. But you're young; I'm not.

MRS BROWN: Tea, David?

DAVID: No, thank you, Mother. A sandwich, please.

TOM: Susan swims very well. After tea, we'll go in again.

SUSAN: Where shall we swim to?

TOM: To that large boat. We'll get into the boat, then we'll swim back to the sand.

DAVID: Where's Toby?

MR BROWN: Under my chair. He's asleep in the sun. He always likes the warm sand.

MRS BROWN: Another sandwich, Tom?

TOM: No, thank you, Mrs Brown. Now I'm going into the
     water. Are you coming, Susan?

SUSAN: Yes. I'll get to the sea before you!

            (*They run down to the sea*)

MRS BROWN: David, we'll take the tea-cups back to the shop.

DAVID: No, Mother, I'll take the tray back.

MRS BROWN: Good boy! Then I'll sit here and read in the
     sunshine.

MR BROWN: And I'll smoke a cigarette. At five o'clock we'll
     drive back to Bishopton.

SENTENCE PATTERNS

34.   The Simple Present Tense

Mr Brown goes to London every day.

He works in London.

Mrs Brown works in the house every morning.

David goes to school every day.

He likes his school.

The Browns go to the seaside on Saturday.

They like a day at the seaside.

Mr and Mrs Brown work on Monday.

Mr Brown lives at Bishopton.

The Browns live at Bishopton.

Every day Mr Brown *drives* his car to the station.

He *is driving* his car to the station now.

Every day Mrs Brown *works* in the house.

This morning she *is driving* to town with her husband.

Simple Present	*Present Continuous*
Every day he works.	Now he is working.
Every morning he drives.	This morning he is driving.
On Monday he goes to school.	Now he is going to school.
Porters carry bags at the station.	The porter is carrying a bag to the train.

Some boys work hard at school.   The boys are working hard
                                 this morning.

The Browns have breakfast in   Today the Browns are having
their dining-room.   their breakfast in the garden.

Mr Brown buys a newspaper   Mr Brown is buying a news-
every morning.   paper at the station.

35.   How Old?

How old is David?   David is seventeen years old.
                                He is seventeen.

How old is Susan?   Susan is nineteen years old.
                                She is nineteen.

How old are you, Tom?   I am twenty years old.
                                I am twenty.

How old is Toby, the dog?   The dog is two years old.
                                The dog is two.

NEW WORDS

ball (boːl)   Sunday ('sʌndi)
boat (bout)   Monday ('mʌndi)
country ('kʌntri)   Tuesday ('tjuːzdi)
cricket ('krikit)   Wednesday ('wenzdi)
deck-chair ('dek'tʃeə)   Thursday ('θəːzdi)
sand (sand)   Friday ('fraidi)
sandwich ('sandwidʒ)
seaside ('siːsaid)
shop (ʃop)   finish, finished ('finiʃ, 'finiʃd)
sky (skai)   fish, fished (fiʃ, fiʃt)
sun (sʌn)   hold, held (hould, held)
  sunshine ('sʌnʃain)   like, liked (laik, laikt)
tray (trei)   live, lived (liv, livd)
water ('woːtə)   shine, shone (ʃain, ʃon)
year (jiə)   smoke, smoked (smouk,
                                  smoukt)
Bishopton ('biʃəptən)   swim, swam (swim, swam)

after ('aːftə)

always ('oːlwəz, 'oːlweiz)

another (ə'nʌðə)

asleep (ə'sliːp)

before (bi'foː)

eighteen ('ei'tiːn)

everyone ('evriwʌn)

except (ik'sept)

far (faː)

often ('ofn)

old (ould)

ready ('redi)

seventeen ('sevn'tiːn)

sometimes ('sʌmtaimz)

then (ðen)

tired ('taiəd)

twenty ('twenti)

young (jʌŋ)

Idioms

seventeen years old ('sevn'tiːn jiəz 'ould)

at the seaside (ət ðə 'siːsaid)

EXERCISES

A. *Answer these questions:*

1. How did the Browns come to the seaside?
2. What are David and Mr Brown doing on the sand?
3. Where is Mrs Brown sitting?
4. Where are the Browns this afternoon?
5. Where will Mr Brown go on Monday morning?
6. How old is David?
7. How old are Susan and her boy-friend?
8. What is the dog doing?
9. Where did Susan and Tom swim to?
10. What is the boy holding in his hands?
11. Where did Mrs Brown buy the tea?
12. At what time will the Browns go home?

B. *Put these sentences into the negative:*

The dog *is swimming* in the sea. The dog *isn't swimming* in the sea.

1. Mrs Brown is playing cricket on the sand.
2. David swam to the big boat.

3. Mr Brown got the tea from the little shop.
4. The Browns will go home by train.
5. Mr Brown and David are sitting on the sand.
6. Susan and her friend swam in the sea.
7. Mr Brown and Mr Brook went to town yesterday.
8. On Friday David came home at four o'clock.
9. Mr Brown saw his friend at the station.
10. Mr Brown bought a newspaper in town.

C. *Put these into the interrogative:*

The Browns are at the seaside. Are the Browns at the
seaside?

1. Susan and Tom will swim to the boat.
2. Mrs Brown is sitting in a chair.
3. The Browns drove to the seaside by car.
4. David and Mr Brown are playing cricket.
5. The dog is asleep under Mrs Brown's chair.
6. Susan will get to the boat before Tom.
7. Mr Brown is smoking a cigarette.
8. Susan swam to the little boat.
9. The Browns will drive home at five o'clock.
10. Susan and Tom were in Bishopton yesterday.

D. *Put words into these sentences:*

1. Toby, the dog, is . . . under Mrs Brown's chair.
2. David and his father . . . playing cricket.
3. Is Susan . . . in the sea?
4. Tom is not . . . the car today.
5. The sun is . . . and the sky is . . .
6. . . . Mr Brown meet his friend at the station?
7. . . . Tom take Susan to town tomorrow?
8. Mr Brown will not . . . to London on Saturday.
9. Every morning Mrs Brown . . . in the house.
10. Mr Brown . . . his car to the station every day.

E. *Put in the Simple Present or Present Continuous:*

1. Mrs Brown (*is drinking, drinks*) a cup of tea on the sand.
2. Mr Brown (*is going, goes*) to London every day.
3. This morning Susan (*is working, works*) in the house with her mother.
4. Every morning Mrs Brown (*is working, works*) in the house.
5. Today Tom (*is taking, takes*) Susan to town.
6. Tom (*is taking, takes*) Susan to town every Saturday.
7. The Browns (*are liking, like*) a day by the sea.
8. In the picture, the children (*are running, run*) across the sand.
9. Mr Brown (*is coming, comes*) home at six o'clock every evening.

F. *Finish these sentences:*

Bishopton is a town . . . London. (*near*)

1. He goes . . . school every day . . . Saturday.
2. Today the Browns are . . . the seaside.
3. The dog is asleep . . . the sand . . . Mrs Brown's chair.
4. The children are running . . . the sand.
5. They will get . . . the boat.
6. They are swimming . . . the sea.
7. Tom will get . . . the sea . . . Susan.
8. David will work hard . . . school.
9. They went to the seaside . . . car.
10. Susan went . . . town . . . Tom . . . his car.

G. *Put these sentences into the singular:*

1. They have some trees in their garden.
2. The boys go to school every morning.
3. The men work in their office in the morning.
4. These boys work hard at school.
5. We live in Bishopton.

LESSON 11

Mrs Brown goes Shopping

TODAY is Monday. Mrs Brown goes to the shops every Monday afternoon. She is shopping in Bishopton now. She is buying some cakes and bread in the baker's shop. The baker sells bread and cakes. Near the baker's shop is the greengrocer's shop. He sells fruit and vegetables: apples, oranges, pears, cherries; cabbages, beans, onions. The greengrocer also sells potatoes. Mrs Brown's friend, Mrs Morton, is in the greengrocer's; she is buying some oranges. She isn't buying apples or pears today.

Mrs Brown goes to the shops on Monday, Wednesday and Friday afternoons. Susan Brown likes cakes; Mr Brown likes salad, but he doesn't like onions. Mr Brown isn't at home now; he is working in London. David Brown is at school.

Mr Stephens, the baker, is always very polite to his customers. "The customer is always right," he says. But his cakes are not always fresh and sometimes his bread is dry. Mr Jones, the greengrocer, is not so polite, and sometimes he gives the wrong change. But his fruit and vegetables are always fresh and his shop is very clean.

In the street outside the shops a man is getting out of a car. He has a bag in his hand; he is going into a bank. In the street a policeman is standing among the cars, motor-cycles and bicycles. In England cars drive on the left-hand side of the street; in many countries they drive on the right. Outside the baker's shop is a van. The driver takes bread and cakes to the houses in the town each day. Bishopton is a busy little town.

CONVERSATION

MRS BROWN (*at the baker's*): Good afternoon, Mr Stephens. I want two white loaves and one brown loaf, please. Your van-driver didn't bring the bread this morning.

BAKER: I'm very sorry, Mrs Brown. He's a new driver. He doesn't know all the houses. Will you take the bread with you?

MRS BROWN: Yes, please. It's for tea today. What cakes have you?

BAKER: The cakes in the window are nice.

MRS BROWN: Are they fresh? Do you make your cakes every morning?

BAKER: Yes, madam. So they're always fresh.

Mrs Brown: I'll have one large cake and a dozen small cakes. How much is that?

Baker: The large cake is twenty-five pence and the small cakes are two pence each. That makes forty-nine pence.

Mrs Brown: Thank you. Here's a pound.

Baker: Thank you, Mrs Brown. Fifty-one pence change. Good afternoon.

. . . . .

Mrs Morton (*at the greengrocer's*): How much are the oranges this morning, Mr Jones?

Greengrocer: Two pence each, madam. Five for ten pence. They're very sweet.

Mrs Morton: I'll take five, please. How much are the apples?

Greengrocer: Five pence a pound the eating apples, and four pence a pound the cooking apples.

Mrs Morton: Two pounds of eating apples, please, and one pound of cooking apples.

Greengrocer: Is that all, madam?

Mrs Morton: Yes, thank you.

Greengrocer: Twenty-four pence, please.

Mrs Morton: Oh, yes. A cabbage and two pounds of beans, please.

Greengrocer: That makes forty pence. Thank you. Will you take them with you?

Mrs Morton: Yes. In this bag, please.

. . . . .

(Mrs Morton *meets* Mrs Brown *in the street*)

Mrs Morton: Hello, Mary! What a nice day!

Mrs Brown: Hello, Joan. How are you? Are you shopping?

Mrs Morton: Yes. I wanted some fruit and vegetables, that's all.

MRS BROWN: Stephens' bread-van didn't bring the bread this morning, so I came into town for it. And some cakes for tea.

MRS MORTON: How're John and the children?

MRS BROWN: Very well, thank you. John's in London to-day. Will you come back to tea?

MRS MORTON: Thank you. That'll be nice. My husband won't be home to tea today.

MRS BROWN: Come on, then! We'll take the bus back. John has the car at the station.

SENTENCE PATTERNS

36. Simple Present Tense—Negative

Mr Brown goes to London on Saturdays.
He does not (doesn't) go to London on Saturdays.
David comes home to lunch.
He does not (doesn't) come home to lunch.
Susan sits in the garden every day.
She does not (doesn't) sit in the garden every day.
Mr Brown goes to London by train; he does not (doesn't) go by bus.
Tom takes Susan to town in his car; they do not (don't) go by bus.
Mrs Brown and her friends go to the shops on Monday; they do not (don't) go every day.
The Browns live in Bishopton; they do not (don't) live in London.
Susan likes a day by the sea; she does not (doesn't) like a day in the house.
David works at school every day; he does not (doesn't) work on Saturdays.

37. Simple Present Tense—Questions

Does Mrs Brown go to the shops every day?   Yes, she does.
                                             No, she doesn't.

Does Mr Brown drive to the station every morning?	Yes, he does. No, he doesn't.
Does David eat his lunch at school?	Yes, he does. No, he doesn't.
Do the Browns work on Saturdays?	Yes, they do. No, they don't.
Do Mr Brown and Mr Brook meet every morning at the station?	Yes, they do. No, they don't.
Do greengrocers sell cakes?	Yes, they do. No, they don't.
Does Susan sit in the garden every morning?	Yes, she does. No, she doesn't.

38.   How Much?

How much does an orange cost?	An orange costs two pence.
How much do oranges cost?	Oranges cost two pence each.
How much is an orange?	Two pence.
How much are oranges?	Two pence each.
How much does a box of matches cost?	A box of matches costs one penny.
How much do matches cost?	Matches cost one penny a box.
How much is a box of matches?	One penny.
How much are matches?	One penny a box.
How much does a pound of apples cost?	A pound of apples costs five pence.
How much do apples cost?	Apples cost five pence a pound.
How much is a pound of apples?	Five pence.
How much are apples?	Five pence a pound.

NEW WORDS

apple ('apl)
baker ('beikə)
bean (biːn)
bicycle ('baisikl)
cabbage ('kabidʒ)

cake (keik)
change (tʃeindʒ)
cherry ('tʃeri)
customer ('kʌstəmə)
dozen ('dʌzn)

greengrocer ('griːngrousə)
loaf (louf)
money ('mʌni)
motor-cycle ('moutəsaikl)
onion ('ʌnjən)
orange ('orindʒ)
penny ('peni)
pence (pens)
potato (pə'teitou)
pound (paund)
salad ('saləd)
side (said)
van (van)
vegetable ('vedʒitəbl)

Joan (dʒoun)
Mr Jones ('mistə 'dʒounz)
Mrs Morton ('misiz 'moːtn)
Mr Stephens ('mistə 'stiːvnz)

bring, brought (briŋ, broːt)
cost, cost (kost, kost)

know, knew (nou, njuː)
make, made (meik, meid)
meet, met (miːt, met)
want, wanted (wont, wontid)

among (ə'mʌŋ)
brown (braun)
busy ('bizi)
clean (kliːn)
dry (drai)
each (iːtʃ)
fresh (freʃ)
left (left)
much (mʌtʃ)
new (njuː)
outside ('aut'said)
polite (pə'lait)
shopping ('ʃopiŋ)
sixty ('siksti)
sweet (swiːt)
thirty ('θəːti)
wrong (roŋ)

Idioms

at the baker's (ət ðə 'beikəz)
come on, then! ('kʌm 'on ðen)
five pence a pound (('faiv'pens ə 'paund)
good afternoon (gud 'aːftə'nuːn)
how much is that? ('hau mʌtʃ iz 'ðat)
I'm sorry (aim 'sori)
is that all? (iz ðat 'oːl)
on the left (on ðə 'left)
on the right (on ðə 'rait)
that'll be nice ('ðatl bi 'nais)
that makes sixty-one pence (ðat meiks 'siksti'wʌn 'pens)
what a nice day ('wot ə 'nais 'dei)

NEW ENGLISH MONEY

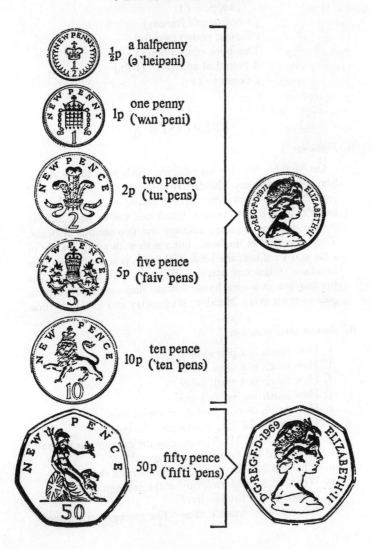

½p — a halfpenny
(ə ˈheipəni)

1p — one penny
(ˈwʌn ˈpeni)

2p — two pence
(ˈtuː ˈpens)

5p — five pence
(ˈfaiv ˈpens)

10p — ten pence
(ˈten ˈpens)

50p — fifty pence
(ˈfifti ˈpens)

100 pence = one pound
100p = £1
£1 one pound (money)
1 lb. one pound (weight)
This book costs a pound (£1)
A pound of apples   (1 lb.)
1 dozen = 12

EXERCISES

A. *Dictation*

On Monday Mrs Brown went into Bishopton to the shops. She goes there every Monday. In the town she met her friend Joan Morton. They went to the greengrocer's and to the baker's. Mrs Brown bought bread and cakes; Mrs Morton bought oranges, apples, a cabbage and two pounds of beans. They didn't go to the bank, but a man with a bag got out of a car and went into the bank. Bishopton is a small town near London. It has one street with shops on each side. The Browns live in a nice house outside Bishopton. Mrs Brown goes to town every Monday, Wednesday and Friday by bus.

B. *Answer these questions:*

1. How much is a pound of apples?
2. How much is a large cake?
3. How much is a small cake?
4. How much are five oranges?
5. How much do two pounds of apples cost?
6. How much did Mrs Brown give the baker?
7. How much did Mrs Morton give the greengrocer for fruit?
8. Where did the man with the bag go?
9. What did Mrs Brown buy at the baker's shop?
10. What did Mrs Morton buy at the greengrocer's?
11. Where do the Browns live?
12. What was the baker's name? The greengrocer's name?

C. *Put these sentences into the negative:*

The Browns *live* at Bishopton. The Browns *don't live* at Bishopton.

1. Mr Brown goes to London each day.
2. Tom Smith takes Susan to town in his car.
3. David works hard at school.
4. Toby, the dog, likes the warm sand.
5. The baker sold all his cakes.
6. The Browns went to the sea in their car.
7. Mr Brown saw his friend at the station.
8. Mrs Morton bought a cabbage at the greengrocer's.
9. David will come home at four o'clock.
10. The children are playing in the water.

D. *Put these sentences into the interrogative:*

1. Susan sits in the garden every day.
2. Mr Brown drives to the station in his car.
3. David works hard at school.
4. Tom and Susan swim well.
5. Mrs Brown went to Bishopton this morning.
6. Tom took Susan to London yesterday.
7. They saw four children on the sand.
8. Mrs Brown and Susan had lunch at home.
9. Mr Brown is sitting in the garden.
10. Toby is a good dog.

E. *Finish these sentences:*

Mr Brown left . . . car at the station. (*his*)

1. Mrs Brown met . . . friend in Bishopton.
2. The Browns drove to the seaside in . . . car.
3. Susan left . . . gloves in the train.
4. I cut . . . hand with a knife yesterday.
5. We carried . . . bags to the train.
6. They are eating . . . dinner in the dining-room.
7. "Where is . . . sister, David?"

8. The dog is eating . . . dinner on the carpet.
9. She took . . . hat and coat from the chair.
10. "Is . . . car at the station, Mr Brown?"

F. *Write ten sentences about Bishopton:*

the street, the shops, where it is, etc.

G. *Finish these sentences:*

Mr Brown went to the station . . . his friend. (*with*)

1. The baker's shop is . . . the station.
2. David Brown is . . . school.
3. The man left his car . . . the bank.
4. In England cars drive . . . the left side . . . the street.
5. These oranges are five . . . ten pence.
6. Mrs Brown went . . . the greengrocer's.
7. The van came . . . the corner.
8. He goes to school every morning . . . breakfast.
9. She took the book . . . the table and gave it . . . her friend.
10. The children ran . . . the sea.

GRAMMAR SUMMARY 1

NOUNS

Nouns (Names)

> boy, girl, book, station, seaside, sunshine, John, London are nouns.

Number: *Singular* = one (*a book*; *the station*).

Plural = two, three, etc. (*two books*; *some books*; *the books*).

Plural of Nouns

1. Most nouns add *-s* for the plural:

book	*books* (buks)
hand	*hands* (handz)
glove	*gloves* (glʌvz)
train	*trains* (treinz)
boy	*boys* (boiz)

2. Nouns with *-s*, *-ch*, *-sh*, *-x* at the end add *-es*:

bus	*buses* ('bʌsiz)
glass	*glasses* ('glɑːsiz)
match	*matches* ('matʃiz)
lunch	*lunches* ('lʌntʃiz)
box	*boxes* ('boksiz)

3. Some nouns with *-f*, *-fe* at the end change to *-ves*:

wife	*wives* (waivz)
knife	*knives* (naivz)
loaf	*loaves* (louvz)

4. Some nouns with consonant + y at the end change *y* to *i* and add *-es*:

country	*countries* ('kʌntriz)
cherry	*cherries* ('tʃeriz)

5. Some nouns with *-o* at the end add *-es*:

potato	*potatoes* (pə'teitouz)

6. Some nouns change a letter in the plural, but do not add -*s*:

man	*men* (men)
woman	*women* ('wimin)
foot	*feet* (fiːt)

7. Some nouns have irregular plurals:

child	*children* ('tʃildrən)
penny	*pence* (pens)

A AND *AN* WITH NOUNS

We use *an* before vowels: a, e, i, o, u:

an arm, *an* afternoon, *an* apple, *an* evening, *an* office, *an* overcoat, *an* orange, *an* onion, *an* umbrella.

We use *a* before consonants: b, c, d, f, g, etc:

a man, *a* woman, *a* book, *a* room, *a* door, *a* window, *a* chair, *a* picture.

We say *the* (ði) before vowels, *the* (ðə) before consonants:

the arm (ði aːm)   the leg (ðə leg)

ADJECTIVES

Adjectives go with nouns. We put an adjective before the noun, or after the verb *Be*:

David is a *tall* boy.	David is *tall*.
Susan is a *pretty* girl.	Susan is *pretty*.
They have a *big* house.	The house is *big*.
We saw a *small* dog.	The dog was *small*.
This is a *warm* coat.	This coat is *warm*.
A *fat* man was sitting in the corner.	The man was *fat*.
A *blue* bird was singing in the tree.	The bird was *blue*.

Other adjectives are:

angry, black, cold, hungry, short, thin, fast, slow, sorry, late, hurt, many, nice, happy, empty, little, ready, young, new, fresh, sweet, right, wrong, clean, polite, dry, busy.

VERBS

TENSE. Tense is time: Present Tense, Past Tense, Future Tense.

The Verbs *BE* and *HAVE*

PRESENT TENSE

be	I	*am*
	he, she, it	*is*
	we, you, they	*are*
have	I, we, you, they	*have*
	he, she, it	*has*

PAST TENSE

be	I, he, she, it	*was*
	we, you, they	*were*
have	I, he, she, it, we, you, they	*had*

FUTURE TENSE

be	I, we	*shall be*
	he, she, it, you, they	*will be*
have	I, we	*shall have*
	he, she, it, you, they	*will have*

PRESENT CONTINUOUS TENSE

This Tense says what I am doing now.
We use the Present Tense of *be* and the verb in *-ing*.

> I *am working*
> He *is going*
> We *are speaking*
> You *are running*
> They *are stopping*

SIMPLE PRESENT TENSE

This Tense says what I always do, what I do every day.

I, we, you, they *work*	he, she, it *works*
play	*plays*
cross	*crosses*
carry	*carries*

Irregular Verbs

I, we, you, they *go*   he, she, it *goes*
         do   *does*

SIMPLE PAST TENSE

Regular Verbs add *-ed* or *-d* to the Present Tense.

Present Tense	Past Tense
work	I, he, we, you, they *worked*
walk	*walked*
close	*closed*
shout	*shouted*
play	*played*
live	*lived*
cross	*crossed*
stop	*stopped*
carry	*carried*

Irregular Verbs

Present Tense	Past Tense
sit	I, he, we, you, they *sat*
stand	*stood*
eat	*ate*
speak	*spoke*
say	*said*
take	*took*
drive	*drove*
go	*went*
do	*did*
come	*came*
leave	*left*
get	*got*
run	*ran*
buy	*bought*
break	*broke*
fall	*fell*
write	*wrote*

see	saw
swim	swam
shine	shone
hold	held
put	put
cut	cut
hit	hit

FUTURE TENSE

I, we	shall	have, run, work, do, etc.
he, she, it, you, they	will	have, run, work, do, etc.

Note   I, we *shall be.*

But   he, she, it, you, they *will be.*

NEGATIVES

be and *have* (Add *not*).

		Negative	Negative in Conversation
Present	I *am*	I *am not*	I'*m not*
	he *is*	he *is not*	he *isn't*, he'*s not*
	they *are*	they *are not*	they *aren't*, they'*re not*
	I *have*	I *have not*	I *haven't*
	he *has*	he *has not*	he *hasn't*
Past	he *was*	he *was not*	he *wasn't*
	they *were*	they *were not*	they *weren't*
	he *had*	he *had not*	he *hadn't*

Present Continuous of other verbs. Add *not* before the verb in *-ing*:

| he *is working* | he *is not working* | he *isn't* (he'*s not*) working |
| they *are working* | they *are not working* | they *aren't* (they'*re not*) working |

Simple Present. Add Simple Present of verb *do* and *not* to the verb:

I *work*	I *do not work*	I *don't work*
he *works*	he *does not work*	he *doesn't work*
they *work*	they *do not work*	they *don't work*

Simple Past Tense. Add Past Tense of *do* and *not* to the verb:

he *worked*	he *did not work*	he *didn't work*
he *drove*	he *did not drive*	he *didn't drive*
he *ran*	he *did not run*	he *didn't run*
he *came*	he *did not come*	he *didn't come*
he *broke*	he *did not break*	he *didn't break*
he *saw*	he *did not see*	he *didn't see*
he *held*	he *did not hold*	he *didn't hold*

Future Tense. Add *not* to Future Tense of verb:

I *shall be*	I *shall not be*	I *shan't be*
he *will have*	he *will not have*	he *won't have*
we *shall work*	we *shall not work*	we *shan't work*
they *will go*	they *will not go*	they *won't go*
		they'*ll not go*

QUESTIONS

be and *have*

Present	I *am*		*am* I?
	he *is*		*is* he?
	they *are*		*are* they?
	I *have*		*have* I?
	he *has*		*has* he?
Past	I *was*		*was* I?
	They *were*		*were* they?
	he *had*		*had* he?

Present Continuous:

I *am working*	*am* I *working?*
he *is running*	*is* he *running?*
they *are speaking*	*are* they *speaking?*

Simple Present. Add Present Tense of *do* to Present Tense of verb:

I *drive*	*do* I *drive?*
he *drives*	*does* he *drive?*
they *drive*	*do* they *drive?*

Simple Past Tense. Add Past Tense of *do* to Present Tense of verb:

he *worked*	*did* he *work?*
I *drove*	*did* I *drive?*
he *swam*	*did* he *swim?*
he *fell*	*did* he *fall?*

Future Tense:

I *shall go*	*shall* I *go?*
he *will work*	*will* he *work?*
we *shall see*	*shall* we *see?*
they *will run*	*will* they *run?*

PREPOSITIONS

These are prepositions:

in, into, out, inside, outside, on, under, near, to, from, up, down, in front of, behind, between, before, after, with, without, through, round, off, among.

1. He walked *into* the room.   2. He was *in* the room.

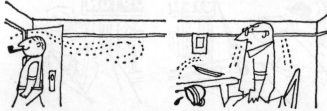

3. He walked *out of* the room.   4. The cup fell *off* the table.

5. The car is *inside* the garage.

6. The car is *outside* the garage.

7. The book is *on* the table.

8. The dog is *under* the table.

9. Mr Brown stood *near* the fire.

10. He stood *in front of* the fire.

11. He is going *to* the station.

12. He is coming *from* the station.

97

13. She went *up* the stairs (upstairs).

14. She came *down* the stairs (downstairs).

15. He was hungry *before* dinner.

16. He was not hungry *after* dinner.

17. The dog stood *between* Susan and David.

18. A van stopped *behind* Mr Brown's car.

19. Mr Brown walked *to* the station *with* his friend.

P.D.E. I—7

20. Mr Brook went *to* work *without* his coat.

21. The man walked *through* the gate.

22. The boys ran *across* the street.

23. The dog ran *round* the tree.

24. She was standing *among* the trees.

NEW WORDS

end (end)
add, added (ad, 'adid)
change, changed (tʃeindʒ, tʃeindʒd)
behind (bi'haind)

between (bi'twiın)
inside ('in'said)
most (moust)
without (wið'aut)

LESSON 12

In the Class-room

HERE is a picture of a class-room at David Brown's school. Bishopton Grammar School is a very good school, and David is happy there. He likes the work and the games. The boys go to school every day from Monday to Friday; Saturday and Sunday are holidays. In the morning school starts at nine o'clock and ends at half past twelve. The boys have an hour and a half for lunch; some boys go home for lunch, some have lunch at school. In the afternoon school starts at two o'clock and ends at half past four. The boys do some home-work in the evening. The homework is about the things they have learned during the day.

On one afternoon each week the boys play games in the field near the school. Many boys also play games on Saturday morning. In autumn, winter and spring they play foot-ball, and in summer there are cricket and tennis.

In this picture, a class is at work in the class-room. This is not David's class; he is seventeen, but these boys are young. The teacher is standing in front of the class. He has a table and a chair beside him, and in his hand he has a piece of chalk. He has a blackboard behind him. The boys are having a lesson. The teacher is speaking to them and point-ing to a map on the wall. The map shows Great Britain: England, Scotland and Wales.

Through the window is the playing-field. Here the boys play football and cricket. David likes games; he is a good footballer and a good cricketer, too. Today some boys are playing cricket. They are in white shirts and trousers and white shoes. One boy is throwing the ball, and the other boy will hit it.

CONVERSATION

TEACHER: This is a map of Great Britain. This is England; this is Scotland; this is Wales. Yesterday I told you the names of some large towns in Great Britain. Do you know them this morning?

BOYS: Yes, sir.

TEACHER: We shall see. Thompson, come here.

THOMPSON: Yes, sir.

TEACHER: Where is London on the map?

THOMPSON: Here, sir.

TEACHER: Right. Now point to Edinburgh.

THOMPSON: Here.

TEACHER: And Cardiff.

THOMPSON: Here.

TEACHER: Now point to Liverpool.

THOMPSON: Here, sir.

TEACHER: Right, Thompson. Thank you. Very good. Sit down.
Now, Barnes. Come here. Point on the map to Glasgow.

BARNES: Here, sir.

TEACHER: No, you're wrong, my boy! Glasgow is here. Now point to Manchester.

BARNES: Here, sir.

TEACHER: Wrong again! Barnes, you didn't listen yesterday. Now try again. Point to Southampton.

BARNES: Here, sir.

TEACHER: That's right at last. Sit down—and today, listen! Now boys, I'll give you an exercise. Put this map into your books. Then write the names of these towns on your maps: London, Edinburgh, Cardiff, Liverpool, Glasgow, Manchester, Southampton.

A BOY: Please, sir. I haven't a pencil.

TEACHER: Take one from my table there.

ANOTHER BOY: Please, sir, my book's full.

TEACHER: Take one from the cupboard.

(BARNES *is talking to another boy*)

Barnes, don't talk. Get on with your work—and do it well or you won't go home at half past four.

BOYS: Oh, sir!

SENTENCE PATTERNS

39.　　　　　Personal Pronouns

Before a verb: *I, he, she, it, we, you, they.*
After a verb or preposition: *me, him, her, it, us, you, them.*

David saw his *friend.*	**He** saw *him.*
Joan met *Susan.*	**She** met *her.*

I saw *David.*	**I** saw *him.*
David saw *me.*	**He** saw *me.*

Mr and Mrs Brown drove *their friends* to the station.	**They** drove *them* to the station.

We met *our friends* and *they* took **us** to their house.

He gave the book **to** *me.*
I took the books **from** *them.*
Come **with** *us* to our house.
Put the flowers on the table **behind** *you.*
I sat **near** *him* on the train.
She stood near the wall and the picture fell **on** *her.*

40.　　　　　Possessive Adjectives

Mr Brown is eating *his* breakfast.
David likes *his* school.
Tom is driving *his* car.
The teacher is standing in *his* class-room.
Susan is writing to *her* boy-friend.
She is sitting in *her* room.
Mrs Brown is cutting flowers in *her* garden.
She is speaking to *her* friend.
The Browns are sitting in *their* dining-room.
Mr and Mrs Brown are talking to *their* children.

The Browns are having dinner with *their* friends.
Susan and David live with *their* father and mother.
David, have you finished *your* homework?
Give me *your* book, Barnes.
Put *your* books on the desks, boys.
We have left *our* car at the station.
We have a big garden round *our* house.

41.   Time—the Quarter Hours

(See Sentence Pattern 33, page 67)

What time is it, please?
It is one o'clock.
It is a quarter past one.
It is one fifteen.   (1.15 A.M. or 1.15 P.M.)
It is half past one.
It is one thirty.   (1.30 A.M. or 1.30 P.M.)
It is a quarter to two.
It is one forty-five.   (1.45 A.M. or 1.45 P.M.)
It is ten o'clock.
It is a quarter past ten.
It is ten fifteen.   (10.15 A.M. or 10.15 P.M.)
It is half past ten.
It is ten thirty.   (10.30 A.M. or 10.30 P.M.)
It is a quarter to eleven.
It is ten forty-five.   (10.45 A.M. or 10.45 P.M.)

NEW WORDS

autumn ('oɪtəm)
blackboard ('blakboɪd)
chalk (tʃoɪk)
class (klaɪs)
   class-room ('klaɪsrum)
cricketer ('krikitə)
cupboard ('kʌbəd)

field (fiːld)
footballer ('futboɪlə)
half (haɪf)
holiday ('holidi)
homework ('houmwəɪk)
lesson ('lesn)
map (map)

pencil ('pensl)
piece (piːs)
playing-field ('plaiiŋfiːld)
shirt (ʃəit)
shoe (ʃuː)
spring (spriŋ)
summer ('sʌmə)
teacher ('tiːtʃə)
tennis ('tenis)
thing (θiŋ)
trousers ('trauzəz)
week (wiːk)
winter ('wintə)
work (wəɪk)

Barnes (baɪnz)
Cardiff ('kaɪdif)
Edinburgh ('edinbrə)
Glasgow ('glazgou)
Great Britain ('greit 'britn)
Liverpool ('livəpuːl)
Manchester ('mantʃistə)
Scotland ('skotlənd)

Southampton (sau'θamtən)
Thompson ('tomsən)
Wales (weilz)

end, ended (end, 'endid)
learn, learned (ləɪn, ləɪnd, ləɪnt)
listen, listened ('lisn, 'lisnd)
point, pointed (point, 'pointid)
show, showed (ʃou, ʃoud)
tell, told (tel, tould)
throw, threw (θrou, θruː)
try, tried (trai, traid)

beside (bi'said)
during ('djuəriŋ)
fifteen ('fif'tiːn)
full (ful)
last (laɪst)
them (ðem, ðəm)
thirty ('θəɪti)
us (ʌs, əs)

Idioms

at last (ət 'laɪst)
at work (ət 'wəɪk)
get on with your work ('get 'on wið jɔɪ 'wəɪk)
sit down (sit 'daun)
you're right (juə 'rait)
you're wrong (juə 'roŋ)

EXERCISES

A. *Write answers to these questions:*

1. What do schoolboys in England play in summer?
2. What do they play in winter?
3. Did Thompson give the right answers to the teacher?
4. Is Glasgow in England or in Scotland?
5. Is Cardiff in Scotland or in Wales?
6. What are the boys in the field doing?
7. When do English schoolboys start work in the morning?
8. When do they have lunch?
9. When do they go home in the afternoon?
10. What do some boys do on Saturdays?
11. What are the boys in the class-room having?
12. What map is on the wall of the class-room?

B. *Finish these sentences:*

1. Don't . . . that pencil from the table, David.
2. . . . swim in the water on a cold day.
3. David and his father . . . playing cricket on the sand.
4. Manchester is a large town in . . .
5. Edinburgh and Glasgow are in . . .
6. Mr Brown . . . to the station yesterday in his car.
7. Did David . . . to school last Monday?
8. David . . . go to school on Saturdays.
9. . . . Tom take Susan to town tomorrow?
10. . . . Susan put the flowers in the dining-room yesterday?

C. *Write sentences with these words in them; one sentence for each word:*

1. cricket; 2. Cardiff; 3. car; 4. bus; 5. dinner; 6. point;
7. meet; 8. breakfast; 9. flowers; 10. book.

D. *Make these sentences negative:*

1. Come here, David.
2. Do this work.

3. Stop that bus.
4. Sit down.
5. Go to school this morning.
6. Put the map on the table, David.
7. Take the pencil from that cupboard.
8. Throw the ball to David, Susan.
9. Put the oranges in my bag.
10. Drive Susan to town, Tom.

E. *Make these sentences plural:*

1. The boy gave a book to his friend.
2. The girl gave the flower to her mother.
3. He doesn't like this house.
4. I shan't read this book today.
5. I took my friend to town in my car.
6. Does he know the man in that shop?
7. Has he read this book?
8. The cup isn't on the table.
9. The boy is putting a map into his book.
10. The man is standing on the platform and the porter is closing the door.
11. He took a match from the box and gave it to the child.
12. His wife has a nice flower in her coat.

F. *Change the verbs in these sentences into the Present Continuous Tense:*

1. David took a pencil from the table.
2. Susan swam in the water.
3. Tom drove to town in his car.
4. Mr Brown met his friend at the station.
5. Mr Brook bought a newspaper.
6. The greengrocer put the oranges in the bag.
7. Mrs Brown and her friend went to the shops.
8. David worked in school.
9. The policeman stopped the cars in the street.

10. David and his father played cricket.
11. Some boys and girls came into the room.

G. *Change the verbs in these sentences into the Simple Past Tense:*

1. Mr Brown is driving his car.
2. Mr Brook is speaking to his friend.
3. The teacher is pointing to the map.
4. Susan and Tom are swimming in the water.
5. Mrs Brown is buying cakes at the baker's.
6. The boy is taking the pencil from the table.
7. The children are crossing the street.
8. Susan is sitting on a chair in the garden.
9. The girls are running into the water.
10. Mr Brown is coming through the door.

H. *Put in the right possessive adjective:*

my, his, her, our, your, their.

1. David gave a book to . . . sister.
2. Susan went to town with . . . boy-friend.
3. I am driving . . . father to the station.
4. We have some nice flowers in . . . garden.
5. David, you have done . . . work well.
6. Mr and Mrs Brown are sitting in . . . garden.
7. Is this . . . book on the table, Susan?
8. David is playing cricket with . . . friends.
9. Tom is taking Susan to the seaside in . . . car.
10. Susan left . . . coat and hat in the garden.

I. *Use these words as prepositions in sentences:*

in, into, under, near, down, after, between, behind, with, across, round, up.

J. *Make these sentences singular:*

1. They live near London.

2. The boys gave the right answers.
3. His friends come to see David every Saturday.
4. We have some flowers in our hands.
5. Do they live in those small houses by the sea?
6. They like eggs for breakfast.
7. The girls start their work at nine o'clock.
8. The children are playing on the sand.
9. The boys play cricket with their fathers.
10. We do not like milk in our tea.

LESSON 13

At Susan's Office

SUSAN BROWN works in an office. She is secretary to Mr Robinson, the manager of a factory. In this factory the workers make clothes: suits for men and coats and skirts for women.

In this picture she is sitting at her desk in the office. On the desk are a typewriter, some pieces of paper and some flowers. She is typing a letter for Mr Robinson. At the office Susan wears a dark skirt, a white blouse and black shoes.

Mr Robinson, the manager, is sitting at his desk in his

room. He is reading a letter. He is a tall man, wearing a blue suit and a red tie. His hair is brown. On his desk are books, papers and a telephone.

Every morning from Monday to Friday Susan comes to the office at nine o'clock. First she opens Mr Robinson's letters. At ten o'clock Mr Robinson rings the bell on his desk and Susan goes into the manager's office with the letters. He gives her the answers to the letters and she writes them in her book. She then goes back to her desk and starts to type.

At eleven o'clock she makes some coffee and takes a cup to Mr Robinson. She then types letters or does other work until half past twelve. Sometimes she goes home to lunch, sometimes she has lunch with her friend, Tom Smith. She works in the office in the afternoon, too, and at five o'clock she stops work and goes home.

Susan likes to be in the office early each morning, but this morning she was late. She came to the office at half past nine. Mr Robinson was angry, and Susan was very sorry. She will work hard all day, and this evening she will work until half past five.

Every month Mr Robinson goes away for two or three days to London or Manchester or Glasgow or Leeds. Then he asks Susan to look after the office. In the evenings Mr Robinson and his wife like to go to the theatre, and sometimes they ask Susan and her boy-friend, Tom Smith, to go with them.

CONVERSATION

MR ROBINSON (*at the door of his office*): Did you hear the bell, Miss Brown?

SUSAN: No, Mr Robinson. It didn't ring.

MR ROBINSON: Perhaps it isn't working. I'll ask the porter to mend it. Are my letters there?

SUSAN: Yes, Mr Robinson. I'll bring them in.

MR ROBINSON: You were late this morning, Miss Brown.

SUSAN: Yes, I was. I'm very sorry. Our clock at home was wrong, and my watch stopped in the night. I'll work this afternoon until half past five.

MR ROBINSON: All right. Don't be late again tomorrow.

SUSAN: No, Mr Robinson.

MR ROBINSON: How many letters have you?

SUSAN: Fifteen. Eight are important.

MR ROBINSON: I'll read those now. Sit down, please, and take down the answers. We'll answer the others this afternoon. I'm waiting for a visitor, a Mr Randall. Bring him in here, please.

SUSAN: Very well, Mr Robinson.

MR ROBINSON: Where's my pen?

SUSAN: That's yours on the desk. This is mine in my hand.
                    (*The telephone rings*)

MR ROBINSON: Answer that, please.

SUSAN (*picking up the telephone*): Robinson and Company. Yes. Mr Robinson is here. One moment, please. (*To Mr Robinson*) For you, Mr Robinson.

MR ROBINSON: Thank you. (*Taking the telephone*) Robinson here—Yes—You'll have nine dozen?—Good—Yes, they're very good. All our clothes are good—All right. On Tuesday, yes. Thank you. Good-bye.
    (*To Susan*) That was Jones and Company, Cardiff. They want nine dozen women's coats.

SUSAN: Shall I write to them?

MR ROBINSON: Yes, please. That's all for now. My wife and I have tickets for the theatre this evening. Will you and Tom come with us?

SUSAN: Thank you, Mr Robinson. I'll telephone Tom now. We both like the theatre and we like to go with you and Mrs Robinson.

MR ROBINSON: Good. Now make some coffee, please. I'm thirsty.

SENTENCE PATTERNS

42. Verb and Infinitive

Mr Robinson likes to go to the theatre.
Mr Brown wants to go to London today.

Mrs Brown is asking Susan to pick some flowers.
The teacher is telling David to take a pencil from the table.

Susan is going to see Mr Robinson.
The boy is running to stop the bus.
Mr Brown drove to the station to meet his friend.
Mrs Brown went to the baker's to get some bread.
Mrs Morton will go to the greengrocer's to buy some oranges.
David ran to meet his friend.

43. Possessive Pronouns
(See Sentence Pattern 40, page 102)

This is *my* book.	This book is *mine*.
That is *your* pencil.	That pencil is *yours*.
This is *his* coat.	This coat is *his*.
Those are *her* flowers.	Those flowers are *hers*.
These are *their* books.	These books are *theirs*.
These are *our* children.	These children are *ours*.
Is that *his* car?	Is that car *his*?
Are those *your* letters?	Are those letters *yours*?
Are these *their* pencils?	Are these pencils *theirs*?
Where is *your* pen?	This is *mine*; that is *yours*.
	I have *mine* in *my* hand; *yours* is on the desk.

NEW WORDS

bell (bel)
blouse (blauz)
clock (klok)
clothes (klouðz)
company ('kʌmpəni)
desk (desk)
factory ('faktəri)
moment ('moumənt)
month (mʌnθ)
secretary ('sekritri)
skirt (skəːt)
suit (sjuːt)
theatre ('θiətə)
telephone ('telifoun)
tie (tai)
typewriter ('taipraitə)
visitor ('vizitə)
watch (wotʃ)
worker ('wəːkə)

Leeds (liːdz)
Miss (mis)
Randall ('randl)
Robinson ('robinsn)

hear, heard (hiə, həːd)

look, looked (luk, lukt)
mend, mended (mend, 'mendid)
pick, picked (pik, pikt)
ring, rang (riŋ, raŋ)
telephone, telephoned ('telifoun, 'telifound)
type, typed (taip, taipt)
wait, waited (weit, 'weitid)
wear, wore (weə, woː)

both (bouθ)
dark (daːk)
early ('əːli)
first (fəːst)
hers (həːz)
important (im'poːtnt)
mine (main)
ours (auəz)
perhaps (pə'haps)
theirs (ðeəz)
thirsty (θəːsti)
thirteen ('θəː'tiːn)
until (ən'til)
yours (joːz, juəz)

Idioms

go away ('gou ə'wei)
go back ('gou 'bak)
how many? ('hau 'meni)
it isn't working (it 'iznt 'wəːkiŋ)
look after ('luk 'aːftə)
one moment, please ('wʌn 'moumənt 'pliːz)
pick up ('pik 'ʌp)
take down the answers ('teik 'daun ði 'aːnsəz)

that's all for now ('ðatz 'oɪl fə 'nau)
the clock was wrong (ðə 'klɒk wəz 'rɒŋ)
wait for . . . ('weit fə)
we both like (wi 'bouθ 'laik)

EXERCISES

A. *Dictation*

Susan is secretary to the manager of Robinson and Company. Yesterday she came late to the office; her watch stopped in the night. Mr Robinson was angry, but Susan worked until half past five that evening. She doesn't like to come late to the office. Mr Robinson asked Susan and her friend Tom to come to the theatre with him. All the morning Susan typed Mr Robinson's letters on her typewriter. At eleven o'clock she made some coffee and took a cup into Mr Robinson's room. She left the office at half past twelve and went home to lunch.

B. *Answer these questions in sentences:*

1. Where does Susan work?
2. What does she do in the office?
3. At what time does she get to the office in the morning?
4. At what time did she get to the office this morning?
5. Was Mr Robinson angry?
6. When does she stop for a cup of coffee?
7. How many letters did Mr Robinson have this morning?
8. Where will Susan and Tom go this evening?
9. At what time will Susan go home this afternoon?
10. Does Mr Robinson go to London every day?
11. What is on Mr Robinson's desk?
12. Has Susan a typewriter on her desk?

C. *Make questions from these sentences:*

1. Susan came to the office at nine o'clock.
2. Mr Robinson was in his room.

3. Susan and Tom like to go to the theatre.
4. Mrs Brown will go to meet her friend tomorrow.
5. This pencil is hers.
6. The children crossed the street near the policeman.
7. You have a book in your hand.
8. David is playing cricket in the field.
9. The girls are running into the water.
10. Mr Brown goes to London every day.
11. The bell on Mr Robinson's desk is working.

D. *Make these sentences future:*

1. The children swam in the sea.
2. Mr and Mrs Robinson took Susan to the theatre.
3. The telephone on Mr Robinson's desk rang.
4. Mr Brown walked to the station.
5. Mr Brook bought a newspaper at the station.
6. Susan sat on a chair in the garden.
7. David had a cup of tea in his hand.
8. Tom drove his car to the town.
9. The postman rang the bell.
10. The two girls crossed the street.

E. *Make these sentences negative:*

1. The Browns live in Bishopton.
2. Mr Brown is eating his breakfast.
3. Susan went to town yesterday.
4. Mrs Brown will go to the seaside tomorrow.
5. Mr Brown and his friend drive to the station every day.
6. The telephone on Mr Robinson's desk is ringing.
7. Susan typed Mr Robinson's letters this morning.
8. The postman took the letters to Mr Brown's house.
9. This book is mine.
10. That was Tom's car.
11. I have a book on my desk.
12. Mr. Brown's car was in the garage.

F. *Finish these sentences:*

1. David likes to ...
2. Susan wants to ...
3. Mr Brown goes to London to ...
4. Mrs Brown asks David to ...
5. The woman tells the porter to ...
6. David runs to ...
7. Susan comes into the garden to ...
8. Tom does not want to ...
9. Mrs Brown does not like to ...
10. Mr Brown tells David not to ...

G. *Put the right word into these sentences:*

1. David said, "The book on the table is (*my, mine, your*)."
2. "This is (*his, her, our*) house," said Mr Brown.
3. This pen is (*my, mine, our*).
4. (*Theirs, mine, your*) pen is on the table.
5. This nice garden is (*their, our, theirs*).
6. The boy took (*mine, his, ours*) pencil from the table.
7. He drove (*his, yours, ours*) car to the station.
8. This book is (*my, mine, our*), that book is (*her, our, yours*).
9. (*Mine, ours, your*) new coat is very nice.
10. Are these (*hers, yours, her*) new shoes?

H. *Put these words into sentences:*

1. street; 2. takes; 3. happy; 4. down; 5. coffee; 6. make;
7. chair; 8. here; 9. shop; 10. come.

LESSON 14

Tea at a Restaurant

IT is Saturday afternoon. Susan and her friend Tom are in London. They came by train this morning; Susan wanted to do some shopping and Tom wanted to buy a new car. Susan went to Oxford Street, and bought a hat, some gloves, a handbag and some shoes. She also bought some handkerchiefs for her mother, a tie for her father and a pocket-knife for her brother David. Tom sold his old car last week, and today he bought a new one. He will have the new one next week; it is a 'Jaguar' and very smart.

Susan and Tom met at Piccadilly Circus at five o'clock and went to a restaurant for tea. After tea, they will go to the theatre. Now they are sitting at a table in the restaurant and the waitress is bringing their tea. They are hungry, so they are having cold meat and salad as well as tea, bread and butter and cakes. The waitress will put the food on the table, and then Susan will pour the tea. Susan is smiling; she is very happy. She likes to be with Tom and she likes to have a day in London. Tom is happy, too; he likes Susan, and soon he will have a new car!

There are some other people in the restaurant. At the next table to Susan and Tom there is a smart woman with her little boy. She is looking at the other people, so she does not see her little boy playing with a glass. He will drop the glass on the floor in a moment and break it; then his mother will be angry. The waitress is bringing an ice-cream for the boy and a cup of coffee for his mother.

There is a fat man in the corner; he is eating a large plate of cakes and reading a newspaper. At the cash-desk a woman is paying her bill; she is giving the cashier some money. Some people are buying bread and cakes. Outside the restaurant, in the street, it is raining; there is a woman with an umbrella up.

After tea, Tom will pay his bill and he and Susan will leave the restaurant and go to the theatre.

CONVERSATION

TOM: What shall we have for tea, Susan? Are you hungry?

SUSAN: Yes, I am. I walked in and out of shops until I was tired, and this afternoon I went for a walk in the park.

TOM: What did you buy?

SUSAN: I wanted a new coat, but there wasn't a nice one. So I bought a hat and some shoes instead.

TOM: Isn't that a new handbag?

SUSAN: Oh, yes. I bought that, too. My other one is getting old.

TOM: It looks very smart. I'm hungry, too. We'll have a good tea. Shall we have a salad, or something hot?

SUSAN: A salad will be very nice. And some tea and cakes.

WAITRESS: What will you have, sir?

TOM: Cold meat and salad, tea and cakes, please.

WAITRESS: Will you have some bread and butter with it?

TOM: Yes, please.

WAITRESS: Very good, sir. (*She goes away*)

SUSAN: Look at that child at the next table. He'll drop that glass and break it in a moment.

TOM: Yes. And look at that fat man in the corner. He's eating all those cakes.

SUSAN: Tell me about the new car, Tom. When will you get it?

TOM: Next week. It's very smart. It's a 'Jaguar'.

SUSAN: What colour is it?

TOM: Red outside and grey inside. You'll like it.

SUSAN: When shall I see it?

TOM: It's in the window of the shop. We'll look at it after tea. Then we'll go to the theatre.

SUSAN: Good. Here's our tea.

(*The waitress brings the tea*)

SUSAN: Will you have another cup of tea, Tom?

TOM: No, thank you. Shall we go now?

SUSAN: Yes. Call the waitress.

TOM: My bill, please. How much is it?

(*The waitress brings the bill*)

WAITRESS: Fifty-five pence, please, sir.

TOM: Thank you. Here's sixty pence.

WAITRESS: Thank you, sir. Good afternoon, madam.

(*They go out*)

SENTENCE PATTERNS

44.   *There is—There are*

There is a map on the wall.
There is a telephone on the desk.
There is a porter near the booking-office.
There is a book on the table.
There is a policeman at the corner of the street.
There is a typewriter in my office.
There are three boys in the room.
There are some cakes on the table.
There are four cars in this street.
There are some people in the restaurant.
There are some boats on the water.
There are some red and yellow flowers in the garden.
There was a book on the table yesterday.
There was a new car outside my house last night.
There was a pretty girl in the office this morning.
There were ten letters for Mr Robinson yesterday.
There were four chairs in the garden this morning.
There were three friends with Susan in the town on Saturday.
There will be a train to London at three o'clock.
There will be a letter for Susan tomorrow.
There will be a new car in the shop on Monday.
There will be some flowers in the garden tomorrow.
There will be some people in the restaurant at five o'clock.

45.   Impersonal *It*—Weather

It is raining. It's raining.
Is it raining?   It is not raining.
It is a fine day. It's a fine day.
Is it a fine day?   It is not (isn't) a fine day.
It is cold this morning.
Is it cold this morning?   It is not (isn't) cold this
                                  morning.

It is very warm today.
Is it very warm today?
It was raining yesterday.
Was it raining yesterday?

It is not (isn't) very warm
today.
It was not (wasn't) raining
yesterday.

NEW WORDS

bill (bil)
cash-desk ('kaʃdesk)
  cashier (kaʃiə)
colour ('kʌlə)
floor (floɪ)
food (fuɪd)
handbag ('handbag)
handkerchief ('haŋkətʃif)
ice-cream ('aiskriɪm)
meat (miɪt)
people ('piɪpl)
pocket-knife ('pokitnaif)
restaurant ('restərɒŋ)
something ('sʌmθiŋ)
waitress ('weitris)
weather ('weðə)

Jaguar ('dʒagjuə)
Oxford Street ('oksfəd striɪt)

Piccadilly Circus ('pikədili
  'səɪkəs)

call, called (koɪl, koɪld)
drop, dropped (drop, dropt)
pay, paid (pei, peid)
pour, poured (poɪ, poɪd)
rain, rained (rein, reind)
smile, smiled (smail, smaild)

also ('oɪlsou)
fine (fain)
fourteen ('foɪ'tiɪn)
grey (grei)
hot (hot)
instead (in'sted)
next (nekst)
smart (smaɪt)

Idioms

to look at (tə 'luk ət)
paying his bill ('peiŋ hiz 'bil)

EXERCISES

A. *Answer these questions in sentences:*

1. Where did Susan go shopping?
2. Where did she meet Tom?
3. At what time did they have tea?
4. What was the little boy in the restaurant doing?

5. What did Susan and Tom have for tea?
6. How much did their tea cost?
7. How much did Tom give the waitress?
8. Where did Tom and Susan go in the evening?
9. What colour was Tom's new car?
10. What did the woman buy?

B. *Change the verbs in these sentences into the Simple Past Tense:*

1. There is a book on that table.
2. It is not raining.
3. We shall go to London by train.
4. They are having their tea in a restaurant.
5. There are many people in the theatre.
6. It is warm in the sunshine.
7. Will you have your lunch at school, David?
8. David has a book in his hand.
9. Will you go to town with David, Susan?
10. At what time will he go to London?

C. *Put the right words into these sentences from:*

there is; there are; there was; there were; there will be.

1. . . . many people in the theatre this evening.
2. Look! . . . a dog in our garden.
3. . . . three visitors in the office yesterday.
4. . . . a bus to Cardiff at five o'clock this afternoon.
5. . . . a book on the table this morning. Where is it now?
6. In this picture . . . some people standing in the station.
7. After lunch today . . . a game of football in the field.
8. "In a corner of the restaurant . . . a fat man eating a plate of cakes," Susan told her mother.
9. Mrs Brown is shopping in town this morning, so . . . a good dinner for her husband this evening.
10. Last Saturday . . . a car outside Tom's house all day.

D. *Make questions from these sentences:*

1. It is very cold today.
2. Tom and Susan are in the restaurant.

3. They came to London by train.
4. They got to the restaurant at half past five.
5. They swam to the little boat.
6. The train will leave at five fifteen.
7. Susan likes to go to the theatre.
8. It was raining yesterday.
9. They took their friends to the theatre.
10. The waitress is bringing their tea.

E. (a) *Write four sentences telling what Susan likes to do.*

   (b) *Write four sentences telling what David wants to do.*

F. *What are these people doing in the picture? Write one sentence for each:*

   1. Susan and Tom.
   2. The waitress.
   3. The little boy.
   4. The little boy's mother.
   5. The cashier.
   6. The woman near the door.
   7. The fat man in the corner.
   8. The woman with the umbrella.

G. *Change the verbs in these sentences into the Future Tense:*

   1. There are some people in the restaurant.
   2. Susan met Tom at Piccadilly Circus.
   3. The teacher is asking David a question.
   4. It is warm in Mr Brown's car.
   5. They are in the theatre.
   6. Does Susan want to buy a new coat?
   7. David didn't go to school by train.
   8. Mr Robinson is answering his letters.
   9. There are some cars and bicycles in the street.
   10. Did Mrs Brown buy some gloves in town?

The Hole in the Roof

Here is a story about an Irishman.

A friend found Paddy sitting in his house. There was a hole in the roof, and the rain came through on his head.

"Mend your roof, Paddy," the friend said. "The rain is coming through."

"Do you want me to go up there in this rain?" asked Paddy.

"No. Mend it on a fine day."

"But the water doesn't come in then," said Paddy.

story ('stoːri)	roof (ruːf)
Irishman ('airiʃmən)	Paddy ('padi)
hole (houl)	

LESSON 15

At the Theatre

SUSAN and Tom are at the theatre. They often come up to London from Bishopton on Saturday to do some shopping, have a meal at a restaurant and then go to the theatre in the evening.

It is now ten past eight, and they are waiting for the play to begin. The theatre is full, and everyone is talking loudly and laughing and smoking or eating chocolates. Soon the red and gold curtain will go slowly up, the lights in the theatre will go out and the play will begin. Then everyone will be quiet.

In front of the stage is a place for the orchestra. The seats next to the orchestra are the stalls. Above the stalls is the circle, and above the circle are the upper circle and the gallery. The seats in the front stalls and in the circle are expensive; the seats in the gallery are cheap. At the moment the orchestra is playing a gay piece of music, and near Tom and Susan one girl is selling chocolates and cigarettes, and another is selling programmes. In England people smoke in most cinemas and in some theatres.

Last week Tom and Susan saw a sad play; this evening they will see a happy play. Susan didn't like the sad play; she likes to laugh and be happy.

Now it is a quarter past eight; the curtain is going up and the play is beginning. After the play Susan and Tom will go home to Bishopton by train. The last train to Bishopton leaves London at ten past twelve.

CONVERSATION

(*In the theatre*)

SUSAN: What time is it, Tom?

TOM: Ten past eight. The curtain will go up in a minute or two.

SUSAN: I haven't any chocolates. Get some quickly, please. Don't get many; I shall get fat!

TOM: All right. (*To the girl*) Half a pound of those chocolates, please. How much are they?

GIRL: Twenty pence, sir.

TOM: Have you any matches?

GIRL: No, I'm sorry, I haven't.

TOM: Never mind. It doesn't matter.

(*To Susan*) Here you are, Susan. Are these all right?

SUSAN: Yes. Thank you very much.

TOM: I wanted some matches, but she hadn't any.

SUSAN: Never mind. I have some in my bag. Now sit down. The play is beginning.

(*The curtain goes up*)

SUSAN (*looking at the actors and actresses on the stage*): Look at that green dress—isn't it pretty? I saw that dress in a shop in Bond Street last week.

TOM: The girl *in* the dress is pretty.

SUSAN (*quietly*): Ssh! Don't speak so loudly. People are looking at you. Have a chocolate?

TOM: No, thank you.

. . . . .

TOM: Are you enjoying the play?

SUSAN: Yes. It's very funny. That fat old man without any hair on his head, with the pretty young wife looks very unhappy.

TOM: Every fat old man with a pretty young wife looks unhappy.

SUSAN: Will she run away with the tall young man in the grey suit?

TOM: No, I don't think so.

SUSAN: Why not?

TOM: He hasn't any money. Who will buy her pretty dresses and smart hats?

SUSAN: Yes, and chocolates at the theatre, and new cars!

TOM: Ssh! The curtain is going up again.

. . . . .

TOM: Well, that's the last curtain. Did you enjoy it?

SUSAN: Yes, I did. I always enjoy a good laugh.

TOM: It's now half past ten; our train goes at twelve ten. We've time for some supper. Where shall we go?

SUSAN: That restaurant in Soho. You know the one. We
    went there two or three weeks ago.
TOM: All right. It's not far from here. Round the corner.
    I'll get my coat, and then we'll go.

SENTENCE PATTERNS

46.   *Some—Any*

Susan has some chocolates.
Has Susan any chocolates?
Susan hasn't any chocolates.

There are some people in the theatre.
Are there any people in the theatre?
There aren't any people in the theatre.

They smoked some cigarettes.
Did they smoke any cigarettes?
They didn't smoke any cigarettes.

Susan will get some flowers from the garden.
Will Susan get any flowers from the garden?
Susan will not (won't) get any flowers from the garden.

Mrs Brown is buying some oranges.
Is Mrs Brown buying any oranges?
Mrs Brown is not (isn't) buying any oranges.

There were some cars in the street.
Were there any cars in the street?
There were not (weren't) any cars in the street.

47.   Adverbs

Tom is speaking quietly to Susan.
People are talking loudly in the theatre.
The curtain went up slowly.

They ran quickly to the station.
Tom and Susan often go to London on Saturday.
They sometimes visit their friends on Sunday.
Susan always enjoys a day in London.

48.   Time—Minutes

What is the time, please?
It is two o'clock.
It is five minutes past two.
It is five past two.
It is two five.   2.5 A.M. or 2.5 P.M.
It is ten minutes past two.
It is ten past two.
It is two ten.   2.10 A.M. or 2.10 P.M.
It is twenty minutes past two.
It is twenty past two.
It is two twenty.   2.20 A.M. or 2.20 P.M.
It is twenty-five minutes past two.
It is twenty-five past two.
It is two twenty-five.   2.25 A.M. or 2.25 P.M.
It is twenty-five minutes to three.
It is twenty-five to three.
It is two thirty-five.   2.35 A.M. or 2.35 P.M.
It is twenty minutes to three.
It is twenty to three.
It is two forty.   2.40 A.M. or 2.40 P.M.
It is ten minutes to three.
It is ten to three.
It is two fifty.   2.50 A.M. or 2.50 P.M.
It is five minutes to three.
It is five to three.
It is two fifty-five.   2.55 A.M. or 2.55 P.M.
It is three o'clock.   3 A.M. or 3 P.M.

NEW WORDS

actor ('aktə)
    actress ('aktris)
cinema ('sinəmə)
circle ('səıkl)
curtain ('kəıtn)
dress (dres)
gallery ('galəri)
laugh (laıf)
light (lait)
meal (miːl)
minute ('minit)
orchestra ('oːkistrə)
play (plei)
programme ('prougram)
seat (siːt)
stage (steidʒ)
stall (stoːl)
supper ('sʌpə)

Bond Street ('bond striːt)
Soho ('sou'hou)

begin, began (bi'gin, bi'gan)
enjoy, enjoyed (in'dʒoi, in'dʒoid)
laugh, laughed (laıf, laıft)

matter, mattered ('matə, 'matəd)
mind, minded (maind, 'maindid)
think, thought (θiŋk, θoːt)

above (ə'bʌv)
ago (ə'gou)
any ('eni)
cheap (tʃiːp)
expensive (iks'pensiv)
fifty ('fifti)
forty ('foːti)
front (frʌnt)
funny ('fʌni)
gay (gei)
gold (gould)
green (griːn)
loudly ('laudli)
never ('nevə)
quiet ('kwaiət)
    quietly ('kwaiətli)
sad (sad)
slowly ('slouli)
unhappy (ʌn'hapi)
upper ('ʌpə)

Idioms

at the moment (ət ðə 'moumənt)
have a chocolate? (hav ə 'tʃoklət)
I don't think so (ai 'dount 'θiŋk sou)
I'm sorry, I haven't . . . (aim 'sori ai 'havnt)

in a minute or two (in ə 'minit ə tuɪ)
isn't it pretty? ('iznt it 'priti)
it doesn't matter (it 'dʌznt 'matə)
it's not far from here (its not 'faɪ frəm 'hiə)
never mind! ('nevə 'maind)
next to ('nekstə, 'nekstu)
to come up to London (tə 'kʌm ʌp tə 'lʌndən)
to do some shopping (tə 'duɪ səm 'ʃopiŋ)
to run away with (tə 'rʌn ə'wei wið)
we've time for supper (wiɪv 'taim fə 'sʌpə)

EXERCISES

A. *Dictation*

Susan Brown and her friend Tom Smith often go to the theatre in London. They come up from Bishopton in the morning, do some shopping and then have a meal at a restaurant. Susan likes to go to the theatre; she is a gay girl, and she often smiles and laughs. This evening the play makes them laugh, so Susan enjoys it. They are sitting in the stalls. In front of them is the orchestra and above them are the dress circle and the gallery. The seats in the gallery are cheap, but those in the stalls are expensive. In front of the stage is a red and gold curtain; this is going up, so the play will soon begin.

B. *Answer these questions:*

1. When does a play begin in England?
2. Where are the stalls in the theatre?
3. Did Tom and Susan see a happy play or a sad play?
4. What did Tom buy at the theatre?
5. How much did they cost?
6. Did Tom and Susan go home by bus or by train?
7. Where did Susan see the pretty green dress?
8. Did Susan enjoy the play?
9. Where do Susan and her father and mother live?
10. Do people smoke cigarettes in the theatre in England?

C. (a) *Write four sentences saying what Mr Brown told David to do.*

   (b) *Write four sentences telling what Mrs Brown asked Susan to do.*

D. *Put these sentences into the interrogative:*

1. The play begins at half past seven.
2. There are some people talking loudly in the theatre.
3. Mr Brown met some friends at the station.
4. Susan will come home at four o'clock this afternoon.
5. Tom smoked some cigarettes in the theatre.
6. The fat man on the stage was unhappy.
7. Tom is speaking quietly to Susan.
8. The Browns have some pretty flowers in their garden.
9. The people in the theatre talked loudly.
10. There is a book on the dining-room table.

E. *Put* some *or* any *into these sentences:*

1. Have you . . . oranges in your bag?
2. We saw . . . boys in the water.
3. There aren't . . . cigarettes in my handbag.
4. Did you see . . . flowers in the garden?
5. There were . . . cups and plates on the table.
6. Buy . . . chocolates for me, please.
7. Are there . . . people in the theatre?
8. He will meet . . . friends in London.
9. The young man hasn't . . . money.
10. Susan saw . . . pretty hats in Oxford Street yesterday.

F. *Finish these sentences:*

1. In the theatre the people are talking . . .
2. The curtain went up . . .
3. The greengrocer spoke . . . to Mrs Brown.
4. The boys ran . . . into school.
5. The play is beginning, so Tom speaks . . . to Susan.
6. Yesterday it was raining; . . . the sun is shining.
7. Tom and Susan . . . go to London on Saturday .
8. Today Mr Brown is in London; . . . he will stay at home.
9. David . . . goes to school from Monday to Friday.
10. David . . . plays football on Saturday morning.

G. *Write these times in words:*

3.15; 4.10; 5.25; 6.30; 8.35; 1.20;
10.5; 11.55; 6.40; 9.45 A.M.; 7.50 P.M.

H. *Write ten sentences on the English theatre. (Do not take your sentences from the book!)*

I. *Put the right preposition into these sentences:*

1. This evening Susan and Tom are . . . the theatre.
2. School starts . . . nine o'clock each morning.
3. The boys have an hour and a half . . . lunch.
4. They do some homework . . . the evening.
5. The teacher is standing . . . the class.
6. He has a table and a chair . . . him.
7. There is a blackboard . . . the teacher's chair.
8. The map is . . . the wall.
9. They see the playing-field . . . the window.
10. They put the map . . . their books.

Who Was He?

A man is looking at a picture on the wall. He says to his friends:

"I haven't any sisters or brothers, but that man's father was my father's son. Who is that man in the picture?"

Do *you* know who he is?

LESSON 16

In the Kitchen

IT is Sunday morning in Mr and Mrs Brown's house. You can see Mrs Brown in the picture; she is working in the kitchen. She is cooking the Sunday dinner. On Sunday the Browns have their big meal in the middle of the day; on other days, 'dinner' is in the evening. All the family are at home, and they can have their meal together.

At the moment Susan and David are at church. Bishopton church is not very far from the Browns' house. The church service will finish at half past twelve. Dinner will be ready at a quarter to one, so they must come home quickly; Mrs Brown will be angry if the dinner gets cold.

It is a fine day today and the sun is shining, so Mr Brown is working in his garden. He does not go to the office on Sunday, so he can work in the garden; he enjoys this very much. He grows vegetables and flowers. He brings the vegetables to the kitchen and Mrs Brown cooks them. Today there are potatoes and a cabbage; last week there were potatoes and beans. Mr Brown digs the garden with a fork and a spade. He must cut the grass every week and keep the garden tidy. You can see Mr Brown through the kitchen window.

Mrs Brown is putting the meat and potatoes in the oven. She cooks by gas, but she has an electric iron, an electric washing-machine and an electric kettle. There is an electric clock on the wall; it says half past eleven. Now the meat is in the oven, and Mrs Brown can clean the vegetables and put them in saucepans.

The kitchen is clean and tidy. There are green and white curtains in front of the window and there are many cupboards on the walls. Mrs Brown is wearing a pretty apron. She is a good cook, and her family and friends enjoy her cooking.

CONVERSATION

MR BROWN (*at the kitchen door*): What vegetables do you want for dinner today, Mary?

MRS BROWN: Some potatoes and a nice cabbage, please.

MR BROWN: All right. Do you want any beans?

MRS BROWN: Not today. We had those last Sunday.

MR BROWN: Have you any flowers in the house?

MRS BROWN: No. I haven't. Bring me some for the dining-room and the sitting-room, please.

MR BROWN: What is there for dinner? I'm hungry.

MRS BROWN: Roast beef. Then apple tart. Shall I make some coffee for you now?

MR BROWN: Yes, please. Then I'll go to get the vegetables.

. . . . .

SUSAN (*coming into the kitchen*): Hullo, Mother! Is dinner ready?

MRS BROWN: Yes. I'll put it on the table now. Who was at church this morning?

SUSAN: Mrs Morton, the Jones family—oh, and old Mr Campbell. Where's Father?

MRS BROWN: In the garden. He's cutting the grass. He must come in now or his dinner will be cold. You can carry the dishes into the dining-room, Susan.

SUSAN: Tom was in church. He came in his new car; it's very smart.

DAVID: Good. You can take Father and Mother out in it this afternoon.

SUSAN: No, we can't. Tom must work at home this afternoon with his books. He takes an examination next week. But next Sunday we can take you and Father into the country, Mother.

MRS BROWN: Thank you, dear. That will be very nice.

MR BROWN (*coming in from the garden*): Hello, you two. Dinner ready? Good! I must wash and change, and then we'll have it.

MRS BROWN: John! Look at the dirt on your boots. Please take them off. You mustn't bring dirt from the garden into my kitchen; I want to keep it clean.

MR BROWN: I'm sorry, my dear. I'll leave these boots in the garage.

MRS BROWN: Hurry up, then! Dinner's ready.

SENTENCE PATTERNS

49. *Can*

Mrs Brown can cook a good meal.
Mr Brown can grow vegetables in his garden.
You can have your dinner now.
You can drive the new car this afternoon.
The policeman can stop the cars in the street.
Now the children can cross the street.
You can go to London on Monday.

Susan can't (cannot) go to London tomorrow.
David can't (cannot) play football this afternoon.
It is cold, so the children can't swim today.
Tom can't take Mr and Mrs Brown in his car this afternoon.
They're not hungry; they can't eat their breakfast.

Can Susan go to the theatre this evening?
Can Toby come to the seaside in the car?
Can Mr Brown grow good vegetables?
Can he get to the station before twelve o'clock?
What can I have for my dinner?
Where can I buy a packet of cigarettes?
When can you come to tea at my house?

50. *Must*

Mr Brown must wash his hands before dinner.
I must write a letter to my friend.
Susan and David must come home at half past twelve.
Mrs Brown must clean the vegetables for dinner.
David must work hard at school.

Susan must not (mustn't) come late to the office.
The dog must not (mustn't) eat Mr Brown's dinner.
Children must not (mustn't) play in the street.
David must not (mustn't) bring his dog to school.

Must David go to school today?   Yes, he must.
Must he come home at four o'clock?   Yes, he must.
Must Mr Brown wash before dinner?   Yes, he must.
Must I work until half past five today?   Yes, you must.

NEW WORDS

apron ('eiprən)
beef (biːf)
boot (buːt)
church (tʃəːtʃ)
dirt (dəːt)
dish (diʃ)
examination (igˈzamiˈneiʃn)
family ('famili)
gas (gas)
iron ('aiən)
kettle ('ketl)
kitchen ('kitʃin)
middle ('midl)
oven ('ʌvn)
saucepan ('soːspən)
service ('səːvis)
sixteen ('siksˈtiːn)
tart (taːt)

washing-machine ('woʃiŋmiʃiːn)

Campbell ('kambl)

can (kan)
clean, cleaned (kliːn, kliːnd)
dig, dug (dig, dʌg)
grow, grew (grou, gruː)
must (mʌst)
wash, washed (woʃ, woʃt)

dear ('diə)
electric (iˈlektrik)
roast (roust)
tidy ('taidi)
together (təˈgeðə)

Idioms

hello, you two! (heˈlou ˈjuː ˈtuː)
the clock says half past eleven (ðə ˈklok sez ˈhaːf ˈpaːst iˈlevn)
to come in (tə ˈkʌm ˈin)
to take an examination (tə ˈteik ən igˈzaminˈeiʃn)
to wash and change (tə ˈwoʃ ənd ˈtʃeindʒ)
what is there for dinner? (wot iz ðeə fə ˈdinə)

EXERCISES

A. *Answer these questions in sentences:*
    1. What is Mrs Brown putting in the oven?

2. What electric machines has Mrs Brown in her kitchen?
3. What is Mr Brown doing in the garden?
4. Who went to church this morning?
5. What must Mr Brown do before dinner?
6. What does Mrs Brown want for the dining-room and sitting-room?
7. What did Mr Brown bring from the garden for dinner today?
8. Does Mrs Brown cook by gas or by electricity?
9. What must Tom do this afternoon?
10. When can Tom take Mr and Mrs Brown into the country in his new car?

B. *Put these sentences into the interrogative:*

1. Tom can come to tea today.
2. Susan wants to go to the theatre this evening.
3. There are some bicycles and motor-cycles in the shop.
4. Mr Brown likes salad for his tea.
5. Mrs Brown bought some oranges at the greengrocer's last week.
6. Mrs Brown is cooking the dinner.
7. The baker sells bread and cakes.
8. Susan can swim very well.
9. Mrs Morton will go to Birmingham on Friday.
10. Tom has a glass of wine in his hand.

C. *Make these sentences negative:*

1. David plays football every Wednesday.
2. Mrs Brown is sitting in a deck-chair.
3. The dog has a chocolate in its mouth.
4. There are some trees in Mr Brown's garden.
5. Mrs Brown can have some beans from the garden.
6. Susan will go to town this afternoon.
7. Mr Brown bought a return ticket at the station.
8. David puts his father's bag into the car.
9. The dogs will run across the sand into the water.
10. There were some apples on the tree in the garden.

D. *Finish these sentences:*

1. Mr Brook bought a ticket at the . . .
2. Mr Brown put his car in the . . .
3. Mrs Brown cut some flowers in the . . .
4. The Browns are eating their dinner in the . . .
5. David goes to . . . every day.
6. The boys are swimming in the . . .
7. Susan and Tom saw a play at the . . .
8. They had tea in a . . .
9. David went to school by . . .
10. The sun is shining in the . . .

E. *Put these words into sentences, one sentence for each word:*

1. five pence; 2. cabbage; 3. boat; 4. hold; 5. stop; 6. take;
7. quickly; 8. loudly; 9. blue; 10. clean.

F. *Make these sentences plural:*

1. The man took his wife to the theatre.
2. The girl bought a knife and gave it to her brother.
3. The woman bought a loaf and a cake.
4. There isn't a bus at midnight.
5. I am eating a cherry from that tree.
6. There is a potato in this saucepan.
7. I haven't a match in my box.
8. Where is the glass? The girl broke it.
9. I have a cabbage in my basket.
10. The actress looks pretty in her green dress.

G. *Put the right word into these sentences:*

1. I gave the book to (*him, he*).
2. We took the flowers from (*them, they*).
3. This is my friend; I met (*she, her*) at the station.
4. Mr Robinson took Susan and (*I, me*) to the theatre.
5. My father and (*I, me*) saw (*he, him*) in London yesterday.
6. They took (*us, we*) to their house for tea.
7. We sat behind (*them, they*) in the theatre.
8. Tom met Susan and went with (*her, she*) to the seaside.

9. Susan said, "Tom is my boy-friend; he often writes to (*I, me*)."
10. Mr Robinson's secretary gave (*he, him*) a cup of coffee.

H. *Put the right preposition into these sentences:*

1. They make suits . . . men and coats . . . women.
2. Susan is sitting . . . her desk . . . the office.
3. She is typing a letter . . . the manager.
4. The books and papers were . . . the desk.
5. She goes . . . the office every day . . . Monday . . . Friday.
6. She types letters . . . twelve o'clock.
7. Tom and Susan go . . . the theatre . . . Mr Robinson.
8. Mr Brown left his car . . . the bank.
9. Mrs Brown walked . . . the road . . . the baker's.
10. They will go to the theatre . . . tea.

The New Baby

"Aunt Mary has a new baby," a mother told her small daughter.

"What was wrong with the old one?" answered the little girl.

aunt (a:nt)
baby ('beibi)

LESSON 17
At the Post Office

THE Browns have some friends in Switzerland. They are a
brother and sister, the same ages as David and Susan. Their
names are Margrit and Edouard Erling. Last summer David
and Susan spent a week with them in Lucerne, and next
summer the Erlings are coming to England for their holidays.
They will stay with the Browns at Bishopton.

Mrs Brown wants to send a letter to the Erling family, but
she hasn't any stamps. So she is going to the post office to
buy some. In England you can buy stamps from the post
office or from a small machine by the side of a pillar-box.

Sometimes there is a small post office in a shop. The post offices open at half past eight in the morning and close at half past five or six o'clock.

Here is a picture of a post office. Mrs Brown is standing in front of the counter, waiting to buy some stamps. The clerk is talking to a postman; the postman is carrying a bag of letters. The clock on the wall says five to eleven. Mrs Brown wants five three penny stamps and three five penny stamps. The stamp for a letter to towns in Britain costs two and a half pence or three pence; the stamp for a letter to other countries costs five pence. At the post office you can send telegrams. You can also buy postal orders to send money by post.

Now the clerk is giving Mrs Brown the stamps and she is giving him some money. She will put a stamp on each letter and then drop the letters into the pillar-box outside the post office. After that she will telephone her friend Mrs Morton. There are some telephone boxes near the wall under the clock. There is a man in one of these boxes, but two are empty. Mrs Brown will find her friend's telephone number in the telephone book, lift the receiver, get the number, and then put the money in the box.

CONVERSATION

Post Office Clerk: Yes, madam?

Mrs Brown: How much is a stamp to send a letter to Switzerland, please?

Clerk: Five pence.

Mrs Brown: Five three penny and three five penny stamps, please. How much is that?

Clerk: Thirty pence, please.

Mrs Brown: Can you give me some two penny pieces for the telephone, please?

CLERK: How many, madam?

MRS BROWN: Two, please. Here's a five penny piece.

. . . .

MRS BROWN (*telephoning*): Is that Bishopton six five two four?

MRS MORTON: Yes. Mrs Morton speaking.

MRS BROWN: Hello, Joan! This is Mary Brown. I didn't see you having coffee in Bishopton this morning.

MRS MORTON: No. I was busy at home. Brian has a cold, and he didn't go to school this morning.

MRS BROWN: Oh, I'm sorry. Is he ill?

MRS MORTON: No. He's not in bed. He's running round the house. All his toys are on the floor in the sitting-room, and his electric train is on the dining-room table. I can't do the housework and I can't cook the lunch.

MRS BROWN: Never mind. He'll be all right tomorrow. I'm going to have a few friends at the house on Friday evening. Can you and Donald come?

MRS MORTON: Thanks very much. We'll enjoy that.

MRS BROWN: Good. The Brooks and the Thompsons and one or two others will be there.

MRS MORTON: Can you come here for a coffee now? Where are you speaking from?

MRS BROWN: Sorry, I can't. I'm in the post office in Bishopton. I must go home now to make lunch for Susan. She's coming home for lunch today. It'll be something cold. I haven't time to cook anything now.

MRS MORTON: Never mind. Now I must go. Brian's shouting.

MRS BROWN: All right. We'll see you on Friday. Good-bye, Joan.

MRS MORTON: Thanks again. Good-bye.

SENTENCE PATTERNS

51.   Present Continuous for Future

Mr Robinson is going to Manchester tomorrow.

Mrs Morton is coming to the Browns' house on Friday.

Tom is buying a new car next week.

Susan is having a holiday in Switzerland next summer.

The Browns are driving to the seaside next Saturday.

The boys and girls are going home after this lesson.

Mr and Mrs Robinson are taking Susan to the theatre this evening.

Mr and Mrs Brown are having some friends to dinner next
   Tuesday.

52.   How Many?

How many stamps do you want?

How many trees are there in this garden?

How many people were at your house yesterday?

How many lessons do you have each day, David?

How many boys are there in your school, David?

How many people are you taking to the theatre?

How many oranges will Mrs Brown buy at this shop?

How many books did David read last week?

NEW WORDS

age (eidʒ)

air mail ('eə meil)

clerk (klaːk)

cold (kould)

counter ('kauntə)

housework ('hauswəːk)

machine (mi'ʃiːn)

post office ('poust ofis)

postal order ('poustl oːdə)

receiver (ri'siːvə)

stamp (stamp)

telegram ('teligram)

toy (toi)

Brian ('braiən)

Lucerne (luː'səːn)

Switzerland ('switsələnd)

find, found (faind, faund)

lift, lifted (lift, 'liftid)

send, sent (send, sent)

spend, spent (spend, spent)

anything ('eniθiŋ)

few (fjuː)

ill (il)

same (seim)

Idioms

by the side of (bai ðə ' said əv)
We'll see you on Friday (wiːl ' siː juː on ' fraidi)

EXERCISES

A. *Answer these questions in sentences:*

1. How many stamps did Mrs Brown buy?
2. How much does a stamp cost for a letter to a town in Britain?
3. How much does a stamp cost for a letter to another country?
4. How much did all Mrs Brown's stamps cost?
5. How many telephone boxes were there in the post office?
6. What is Mrs Morton's telephone number?
7. When are the Mortons coming to Mrs Brown's house?
8. Who are coming to Mrs Brown's house on that day?
9. Who was at home with Mrs Morton?
10. What is he doing?

B. *Write two short answers to each of these questions:*

Is Mrs Brown in the post office?   Yes, she is.
                                     No, she isn't.

1. Has Mrs Brown a letter in her hand?
2. Are there three telephone boxes in the post office?
3. Can Mrs Brown buy stamps at the post office?
4. Is Susan coming home to lunch today?
5. Is Mrs Brown buying some stamps?
6. Is there a typewriter on Susan's desk at the office?
7. Did Mr Brown take a taxi to the station?
8. Does David go to school every day?
9. Is it raining?
10. Have you been to London this week?
11. Can you speak English?
12. Will you finish your work before lunch?

C. *What are these people doing in the picture?*

    1. The post-office clerk; 2. The postman; 3. The man in the telephone box; 4. Mrs Brown.

D. *Put the right words into these sentences:*

    Today he (*drive*) to the station. (*is driving*)

    1. Yesterday they (*buy*) a new car.
    2. Tomorrow he (*go*) to London.
    3. At the moment the sun (*shine*).
    4. Last week we (*work*) every day.
    5. This morning Mrs Brown (*cook*) the dinner.
    6. Next Saturday the Browns (*drive*) to the seaside.
    7. Every Wednesday David (*play*) football.
    8. In the picture Mrs Brown (*talk*) to the clerk.
    9. Mr Brown (*come*) home at six o'clock every day.
    10. Three days ago Tom (*take*) Susan to the theatre.

E. *Put these words into sentences, one sentence for each phrase:*

    round the corner; on the floor; on the wall; in front of the house; through the gate; into the train; at the table; behind the door; in the room; from his friend.

F. *Write these numbers in words:*

    15; 26; 21; 19; 30; 28.

    Write these times in words:

    6.45 P.M.; 3.20 P.M.; 12.45 A.M.; 4.50 P.M.; 10.30 A.M.

G. *Make these sentences plural:*

    1. I have a box of matches in my hand.
    2. My wife likes to go to the seaside.
    3. Does he live in this house?
    4. He hasn't a flower in his garden.
    5. Where does the boy play cricket?
    6. Has he a tree in his garden?
    7. The bus leaves London at six o'clock.

8. She has an orange and an apple in her bag.
9. There is a cherry on that tree.
10. She is waiting for her friend.

H. *Write these words, adding the letters left out:*

he isn't; he won't; they can't; I shan't; they don't; he didn't;
you aren't; she wasn't; they weren't; we haven't; he hasn't;
you hadn't.

Office Workers

A young man started work in a large Government office.
At the end of his first day, he came home and his father
asked him some questions.

"And how many people work in your office?" he began.

"Oh, about half the people there!" his son answered.

LESSON 18

On the Farm

THE fifth of June was a warm day. Mrs Brown woke up early that morning. She looked out of the window and saw the sun shining and the blue sky. "John," she said, waking her husband, "it's going to be a lovely day today. I think I'll go to see Ethel, and have a day in the country." Ethel is Mrs Brown's sister; she is a farmer's wife who lives on a farm ten miles from Bishopton. John Brown, who was still half asleep, said, "Good. I'll walk to the station; then you can have the car."

Mrs Brown jumped out of bed, dressed, and cooked the family's breakfast. Then she did her housework. And at half-past ten Mrs Brown was driving quietly along a country road between green banks. Birds were singing in the sky, and she heard a dog on the other side of the field. Suddenly, Mrs Brown came round a bend in the road and nearly ran into a cow which was crossing the road. She stopped the car and waited for the cow to cross. It did not hurry! Then she drove on, but more slowly this time. It was a lovely day and she didn't want to hurry.

She left the car near her sister's farm, and soon she was walking through the farmyard to the house. In a corner of the farmyard she saw her sister's husband, Joe Stansbury, the farmer. He was looking at some pigs which he was going to take to market next day. With the money he gets for his pigs he buys winter food for the cows and other animals on the farm. Joe Stansbury is a big man with wide shoulders and a red face. He likes Mary Brown and was very pleased to see her. Ethel Stansbury, his wife, a pretty woman in a clean white apron, was standing at the door of the farmhouse. She, too, was very pleased to see her sister.

The Stansburys have a large farm with many fields. In some fields the farmer grows corn; in others he grows cabbages and potatoes which go to Covent Garden Market in London; Covent Garden is a big fruit and vegetable market. Cows and sheep feed in some fields, and near the house there are apple-trees, pear-trees, plum-trees and cherry-trees. Mrs Brown always enjoys a visit to her sister's farm; it is very different from her home in the town.

CONVERSATION

ETHEL STANSBURY: Hello, Mary. What a lovely day!

JOE STANSBURY: Nice to see you, Mary. Did you come by car?

MARY BROWN: Yes. I left it outside the farmyard gate. It *is* a lovely day. Joe, one of your cows is on the road. I was driving along and nearly ran into it.

JOE: Someone left the gate open. That's the fourth time this week. (*Calling to one of his men*) George!

GEORGE (*coming from behind the house*): Yes, Mr Stansbury?

JOE: There's a cow in the road. Someone left the gate open, and Mrs Brown's car nearly ran into it. Get it in, will you?

GEORGE: All right, Mr Stansbury. I'll see to it.

ETHEL: Now, Mary, come into the house. You must be ready for a cup of tea. Then you can walk round the farm with me; I'm just going to get the eggs.

MARY: Thanks, Ethel. I can do with a cup of tea.

JOE: Excuse me, will you? I must get these pigs into the van. I'm going to take them to the man who bought them from me yesterday.

MARY (*looking at the pigs*): You've some good pigs there, Joe.

JOE: Yes, they're all right. Well, you two go and have your tea and I'll get on with my work. I'll see you at lunch, Mary.

MARY: Thanks.

. . . . .

ETHEL: Here we are! A nice cup of tea. And some cakes which I made this morning.

MARY: They're lovely, Ethel. You're a very good cook.

ETHEL: A farmer's wife must be a good cook. Farmers and their men are always hungry.

MARY: The farm's looking well at the moment. Are you busy?

ETHEL: We're always busy on a farm, from January until December.

MARY: The corn will soon be ready in this hot sunshine.

ETHEL: Next month, in July, we shall cut the grass for hay, and in August or early September we shall harvest the corn. We'll be very busy then.

MARY: David will come for a week or two to help you. He's going to Switzerland for three weeks from the second of August, then he'll come to you to help with the harvest.

ETHEL: Thanks. We'll be pleased to see him. Will you have another cup of tea?

MARY: No, thanks. That was very nice.

ETHEL: Now we'll go to see the chickens. I was cooking this morning, so I didn't get the eggs. We'll go and get them now. Then you can have some to take home with you.

MARY: Thanks very much. John and the children like eggs from the farm. How many chickens have you now?

ETHEL: A hundred and fifty. You can have one for your Sunday dinner.

MARY: You're very good. Now I'll help you get the eggs. Where shall we start?

ETHEL: In the chicken-houses; there'll be a lot of eggs there. Then we'll look under the trees. I often find eggs there. I'll take this basket, and here's one for you. We'll come back for the third one later. It's going to be hot, so we'll put our hats on.

SENTENCE PATTERNS

53.   Relative Pronouns—*Who, Which, That*

They met a man who has a new car.
Mrs Brown knows a woman who lives in Birmingham.

This is the man who came to the house yesterday.
Do you know the boy who lives in the big house?
It was Mr Brook who came here this morning.
It was Mr Robinson who took Susan to the theatre.
We are looking for the girl who dropped this handbag.
Did you see the boy who broke that window?
I have a book for the boy who answers all these questions.
The people who live in this house are on holiday.

I am looking for the book (which, that) I left on the table.
She is carrying the vegetables (which, that) she bought in the
    town.
These are the eggs (which, that) Mrs Brown brought from the
    farm.
Can I have one of the cigarettes (which, that) you bought at the
    station?
Have you seen the flowers (which, that) Mrs Brown put in the
    sitting-room?
We don't like the cakes (which, that) the baker sells.
The apple (which that) she is eating came from our garden.

54. Past Continuous Tense

The child was crossing the street.
The boy was eating an apple.
Mr Brown was digging his garden.
Mrs Brown was cooking the dinner.
The porter was carrying some bags.
Mr Stansbury was smoking a cigarette.
Tom was cleaning his new car.
The friends were laughing and talking.
They were sleeping in their beds.

55. Future with *Go* and the Infinitive

I'm going to spend a day in the country.
It's going to be a lovely day.

We're just going to have our lunch.
David is going to work hard at school this year.
Tom is going to buy a new car soon.
A woman who eats too many cakes is going to get fat.
It's going to rain tomorrow.
I'm going to sit and read a book all the afternoon.
"Are you going to ask me to dinner?"
"I'm not going to speak to her again."
I'm just going to write a letter to Tom.
We're just going to have a drink.
What are you going to do this evening?
Are you going to come with us?

NEW WORDS

animal ('animəl)
basket ('baːskit)
bend (bend)
bird (bəːd)
chicken ('tʃikin)
corn (koːn)
cow (kau)
farm (faːm)
   farmer ('faːmə)
   farmhouse ('faːm'haus)
   farmyard ('faːmjaːd)
harvest ('haːvist)
hay (hei)
market ('maːkit)
mile (mail)
pig (pig)
road (roud)
sheep (ʃiːp)
shoulder ('ʃouldə)
visit ('vizit)

January ('dʒanjuəri)

February ('februəri)
March (maːtʃ)
April ('eiprl)
May (mei)
June (dʒuːn)
July (dʒuːˈlai)
August ('oːgəst)
September (səpˈtembə)
October (okˈtoubə)
November (nouˈvembə)
December (diˈsembə)

Covent Garden ('kʌvənt
   'gaːdn)
Ethel ('eθəl)
George (dʒoːdʒ)
Joe Stansbury ('dʒou
   'stanzbri)

dress, dressed (dres, drest)
excuse, excused (iksˈkjuːz,
   iksˈkjuːzd)

feed, fed (fiːd, fed)

help, helped (help, helpt)

jump, jumped (dʒʌmp, dʒʌmpt)

sing, sang (siŋ, saŋ)

wake, woke (weik, wouk)

along (əˈloŋ)

different (ˈdifrənt)

eighteen (ˈeiˈtiːn)

fifth (fifθ)

fourth (foɪθ)

hundred (ˈhʌndrəd)

just (dʒʌst)

lot (lot)

lovely (ˈlʌvli)

nearly (ˈniəli)

second (ˈsekənd)

someone (ˈsʌmwʌn)

still (stil)

suddenly (ˈsʌdnli)

third (θəɪd)

which (witʃ)

wide (waid)

Idioms

a lot of eggs (ə ˈlot əv ˈegz)

excuse me (iksˈkjuːz miː)

get it in (ˈget it ˈin)

here's one for you (ˈhiəz ˈwʌn fə ˈjuː)

I can do with a cup of tea (ai kən ˈduː wið ə ˈkʌp əv ˈtiː)

I think I'll go (ai ˈθiŋk ail ˈgou)

I'll see to it (ail ˈsiː tu it)

I'm just going to . . . (aim ˈdʒʌst ˈgouiŋ tə)

nice to see you (ˈnais tə ˈsiː juː)

on the other side of (on ði ˈʌðə ˈsaid əv)

ready for a cup of tea (ˈredi fə ə ˈkʌp əv tiː)

to come round a bend (tə ˈkʌm ˈraund ə ˈbend)

EXERCISES

A. *Answer these questions in sentences:*

1. What was the name of Mrs Brown's sister?
2. Where is the Stansbury's farm?
3. What did Mrs Brown see crossing the road?
4. What did Mrs Stansbury give her sister?
5. Where did Mrs Stansbury often find eggs?

6. Where does Mr Stansbury send his vegetables to market?
7. What does this farmer grow in his fields?
8. When will the farmer and his men be very busy?
9. What will the farmer buy when he sells his pigs?
10. Where is David going for his holidays next summer?

B. *Write ten sentences about the Stansburys' farm.* (*Do not take the sentences from the book.*)

C. *Put* who *or* which *into these sentences:*
   1. This is the house . . . has a large garden.
   2. The boy . . . lives next door broke a window.
   3. Mrs Brown was speaking to the man . . . brings the bread.
   4. The letter . . . came this morning was for Susan.
   5. Susan, . . . works in an office, starts work at nine o'clock.
   6. Where is the letter . . . came this morning?
   7. We don't like the postman . . . brings our letters.
   8. Did you see the visitor . . . was here this afternoon?
   9. There is the book . . . was on the table.
   10. The teacher gave a book to the boy . . . answered all the questions.

D. *Write ten sentences beginning with* "How many . . .?" (*Not the sentences on page* 146.)

E. *Put these sentences into the interrogative:*
   1. Mary Brown is spending a day in the country.
   2. She likes to visit her sister on the farm.
   3. She drove her car slowly along the road.
   4. The birds were singing in the sky.
   5. She will bring home some eggs for the family.
   6. David is going to Switzerland in August.
   7. There was a cow crossing the road.
   8. It was raining last Saturday.
   9. There will be some eggs in the chicken-house.
   10. There were some sheep in the field.

F. *Use each of these idioms in a sentence; one sentence for each:*

1. Good-bye 2. Thank you 3. Hello 4. How are you?
5. Good morning 6. Here we are 7. All right 8. At home
9. At the seaside 10. Six years old.

G. *Put the right word into these sentences:*

1. David (*goes, is going*) to school every day.
2. Mrs Brown (*likes, is liking*) to visit her sister.
3. It is a fine day, and Mrs Brown (*is driving, drives*) slowly along the road.
4. Mrs Brown is in the farmyard and she (*talks, is talking*) to her sister.
5. The Browns (*go, are going*) to church every Sunday.
6. The farmer (*takes, is taking*) his pigs to market every week.
7. Now Mary and Ethel (*get, are getting*) the eggs from the chicken-house.
8. This afternoon Tom (*is working, works*) for his examination.
9. Mr Brown always (*drives, is driving*) to the station in his car.
10. At the moment Mrs Brown (*makes, is making*) cakes in the kitchen.

H. *Write sentences with these verbs in the Simple Past Tense:*

find: She found an egg in the hen-house.

sit; eat; speak; take; come; leave; buy; fall; swim; hold; run; write.

I. *Put the verbs in these sentences into the Future Tense, using* Go:

1. He will sell all his pigs tomorrow.
2. It will be a lovely day today.
3. They will have a holiday in Switzerland next year.
4. He will work all tomorrow.
5. She will write to her friend.
6. David will play football on Saturday.

7. Will you stay to tea?
8. Will she look round the farm?
9. He will take his pigs to market.
10. Will she finish that letter before dinner?

The Farmer Comes to Town

A farmer and his wife from the country were in London for the first time. They saw in the window of a restaurant:

"LUNCHES—12 until 2. 25p"

"Come on, Mary," said the farmer, "that's cheap. We can sit here and eat for two hours for twenty-five pence."

LESSON 19

A Visit to London

MARGRIT and Edouard Erling, the Browns' two young friends from Switzerland, were staying with them at Bishopton. The Erlings did not know London, so Susan and David took them to visit the West End and the City.

The City is quite small, but it is very important. Two thousand years ago the Romans built a town here. For hundreds of years people lived and worked here, but now nearly all the old houses have gone. Instead, there are large offices. Thousands of people come here by train every morning, and in the evening they go home again. At night the City is very quiet and empty.

In the West End there are theatres, cinemas, long streets of fine shops and many big houses. There are beautiful Parks, too. In the West End you will find most of the offices of the Government.

David and Susan took their friends first of all to Buckingham Palace, the home of the Queen and the Royal Family. The Queen was coming out of the Palace in her car as they arrived, so they saw her. Margrit and Edouard were very pleased; the Queen was one of the people whom they wanted to see while they were in England.

Then they walked down Whitehall, which is the street where all the Government offices are. When they were crossing the road to Westminster Abbey, 'Big Ben', the clock on the Houses of Parliament, struck ten. From Westminster they went down the River Thames by boat to the Tower of London, which is a very old castle. There they saw the big black birds which live in the Tower. They also saw the

Queen's jewels. Then they went into St Paul's Cathedral, which is not far from the Tower, and into some other churches in the City. Near St Paul's they saw the Mansion House, the home of the Lord Mayor of London. Each November there is a new Lord Mayor, and he lives in the Mansion House until the next one takes his place.

After lunch, they got on a bus which took them to the National Gallery. Here they saw many beautiful pictures, and the Swiss boy and girl, whose mother paints pictures, enjoyed their visit very much.

They had dinner in a little restaurant in Soho, to which Susan and her boy-friend Tom often go, and after dinner Susan and David took their Swiss friends to a theatre. Margrit and Edouard know English very well, so they enjoyed the play. It was midnight when they got home after a very interesting day.

CONVERSATION

DAVID: This is Whitehall. All those big buildings are Government offices. At the beginning of November every year the Queen drives down Whitehall from Buckingham Palace to open Parliament. Many people come to watch the Queen and the soldiers who ride with her.

MARGRIT: What are those buildings at the end of the street?

DAVID: You know the building with the clock; that's the Houses of Parliament. The building beside it with two towers is Westminster Abbey. Now we'll go by boat to the Tower.

EDOUARD: How far is it?

DAVID: About three miles. It's near Tower Bridge.

EDOUARD: Is that the bridge that opens in the middle to let boats go through?

DAVID: Yes. Now we're going under London Bridge. This bridge isn't old, but there was a bridge here many years ago with houses and shops on it.

MARGRIT: Is that the Tower of London? But there are lots of towers there.

DAVID: Yes, but the one in the middle—the White Tower—is *the* Tower.

MARGRIT: How old is it?

DAVID: About a thousand years old. Years ago Kings and Queens lived—and died—here.

SUSAN: I don't like the Tower. It's cold and grey, and it frightens me. We'll go and have lunch. I'm hungry.

DAVID: All right. There's an old restaurant near here which you'll like. The food's very good.

• • • • •

MARGRIT: Can we get to the National Gallery from here?

DAVID: Yes. We'll go by bus. Then you can see all the interesting buildings on the way. That's the Bank of England. This is Fleet Street, with all the newspaper offices. Now we're in the Strand. Charing Cross Station is on the left, and now we are coming to Trafalgar Square. The National Gallery is on the right.

MARGRIT: How many pictures are there in the Gallery?

DAVID: About six hundred, I think.

EDOUARD: Don't ask hard questions, Margrit. David doesn't know everything.

MARGRIT: All right. I'll ask an easy question. Where can I wash my hands?

SUSAN: Come on! I'll show you. Down these stairs.

SENTENCE PATTERNS

56. Time Clauses—*When, While, Before*

It was raining when we left the theatre.
The people were talking loudly when the curtain went up.
Susan was typing letters when Mr Robinson rang the bell.
When Mr Brown came home his wife was putting the dinner on the table.

Mrs Brown is pleased to see her husband when he comes home.
David sometimes walks to school when the sun is shining.
David will go to bed when he comes home.
Susan will leave the office when the clock says half past five.
While they were standing near the Palace, the Queen drove out in her car.
They left the theatre before the curtain came down.
Before you have lunch you must wash your hands.

57.   Relative Pronouns—*Whose*

(See Sentence Pattern 53, page 153)

This is the man who lives in the big house.
David was the boy who gave me this book.

He is one of the men we wanted to meet.
Is that the boy you saw at the station?
Do you know the names of the actors you saw on the stage?
This is the man you met last summer.
David wrote a letter to a boy he knows.
Is that the man we saw on television?

I was speaking to the boy whose family live in Cardiff.
The Browns, whose father works in London, live in Bishopton.
He is one of the boys whose father can play cricket well.
I saw the writer whose new play is at the theatre this week.
I spoke to the man whose dog ran into our garden.
This is the woman whose home is in Birmingham.
We met Mr Jones, whose son goes to David's school.

This is the knife (which, that) I took from the table.
Mrs Brown bought the coat (which, that) she saw in the shop-
window.

Give me the book (which, that) you were reading, please.
Susan will open the letters (that) Mr Robinson gave her.

NEW WORDS

beginning (bi'giniŋ)
bridge (bridʒ)
building ('bildiŋ)
castle ('kaːsl)
government ('gʌvənmənt)
jewel ('dʒuːəl)
king (kiŋ)
place (pleis)
queen (kwiːn)

soldier ('souldʒə)
stair (steə)
way (wei)

Big Ben ('big 'ben)
Buckingham Palace ('bʌkiŋəm 'palis)
Charing Cross ('tʃariŋ 'kros)
City ('siti)

Fleet Street (ˈfliːt striːt)
Lord Mayor (ˈloːd ˈmeə)
Mansion House (ˈmanʃn ˈhaus)
National Gallery (ˈnaʃnəl ˈgaləri)
St Paul's Cathedral (sənt ˈpoːlz kəˈθiːdrəl)
Thames (temz)
Tower of London (ˈtauə əv ˈlʌndən)
Trafalgar Square (trəˈfalgə ˈskweə)
West End (ˈwest ˈend)
Westminster Abbey (ˈwestminstə ˈabi)
Whitehall (ˈwaitˈhoːl)

arrive, arrived (əˈraiv, əˈraivd)
build, built (bild, bilt)

die, died (dai, daid)
frighten, frightened (ˈfraitn, ˈfraitnd)
let, let (let, let)
paint, painted (peint, ˈpeintid)
ride, rode (raid, roud)
strike, struck (straik, strʌk)
watch, watched (wotʃ, wotʃt)

beautiful (ˈbjuːtiful)
easy (ˈiːzi)
everything (ˈevriθiŋ)
interesting (ˈintrəstiŋ)
long (loŋ)
roman (ˈroumən)
royal (ˈroiəl)
thousand (ˈθauzənd)
while (wail)
whom (huːm)
whose (huːz)

Idioms

at the beginning of November (ət ðə biˈginiŋ əv nouˈvembə)
at the end of the street (ət ði ˈend əv ðə ˈstriːt)
for hundreds of years (fə ˈhʌndrədz əv ˈjiəz)
how far is it? (hau ˈfaː iz it)
I'll show you (ail ˈʃou juː)
many years ago (ˈmeni ˈjiəz əˈgou)
on the way (ˈon ðə ˈwei)
the clock struck ten (ðə ˈklok ˈstrʌk ˈten)
they got on a bus (ðei ˈgot on ə ˈbʌs)
to let boats go through (tə ˈlet ˈbouts gou θruː)

EXERCISES

A. *Answer these questions:*
  1. How far is the Tower of London from Westminster?

2. How many pictures are there in the National Gallery?
3. How old is the Tower of London?
4. How many pence are there in a pound?
5. What are the buildings in Whitehall?
6. Who lives in Buckingham Palace?
7. What did David and his friends hear when they were crossing the road to Westminster Abbey?
8. Where did they have dinner?
9. At what time did they get home?

B. *Finish these sentences:*

1. The policeman stops the cars when . . .
2. This is the house which . . .
3. Yesterday we were speaking to the girl who . . .
4. They went home before . . .
5. Susan will go home when . . .
6. Did you see the boy to whom . . .
7. We do not know how . . .
8. Is that the teacher from whom . . .
9. She is one of the girls whose . . .
10. Give me the book which . . .

C. *Make these sentences plural:*

1. He had a knife in his hand.
2. That city is very large.
3. A bridge crosses the river.
4. Does he live in this house or in that?
5. I saw a sheep in the farmyard.
6. Will she come to London with me on Sunday?
7. This is the boy whom I met last week.
8. Is my coat here? I left it here this morning.
9. He had a glove on his hand and a shoe on his foot.
10. The child was eating a cherry from my garden.

D. *Put the right preposition into these sentences:*

1. Susan and Tom swam . . . the water.

2. The people walked . . . the gate.
3. Mr Brown is going to London . . . his friend.
4. The car came . . . the corner quickly.
5. The postman was standing . . . the house.
6. The blackboard was . . . the teacher.
7. The children were running . . . the sand.
8. Mr Brown stood . . . the fire.
9. Mrs Brown took the shoe . . . the dog.
10. Mr Brook took . . . his coat when he came . . . the house.

E. *In these sentences put the Present Continuous Tense for the Future Tense:*

1. I shall come to Bishopton on Wednesday.
2. He will have his lunch in school today.
3. Susan and Tom will go to the theatre this evening.
4. We shall stay at home tomorrow.
5. Father will take us to the seaside on Saturday.
6. I shall leave my car outside your house until this evening.
7. Tom will buy a new car next week.
8. She will send some eggs to her friend in London tomorrow.
9. Mrs Brown will bring her husband some new gloves from town this afternoon.
10. Mrs Brown will visit her sister on the farm next Friday.

F. *Make sentences with these verbs in the Imperative:*

Go. Go home now, children.

1. take; 2. come; 3. make; 4. drive; 5. eat; 6. write; 7. close; 8. finish; 9. put; 10. work.

G. *Finish these sentences by adding a noun to the verb:*

1. The Browns were eating . . .
2. Mr Brown is driving . . . to the station.
3. Joe Stansbury is taking . . . to market.
4. Susan typed . . . for Mr Robinson.
5. Mrs Brown bought . . . at the post office.

6. David carries . . . to school each day.
7. Susan is putting . . . in the dining-room.
8. Mrs Stansbury found . . . under the trees.
9. Mr Robinson took . . . to the theatre.
10. Mr Brown took . . . from the station to his office.

H.

(a) *Write three sentences beginning with "How old . . .?"*
(b) *Write three sentences beginning with "How much . .?"*
(c) *Write three sentences beginning with "How many . . .?"*
(d) *Write three sentences beginning with "How far . . .?"*

I. *Put the possessive adjective or pronoun into these sentences:*
1. Tom and Susan met . . . friends at the seaside.
2. We left . . . coats in the car.
3. You must take . . . books to school, David.
4. Susan finished . . . work at five o'clock.
5. That is . . . book, David, and this is . . .
6. The dog ate . . . dinner on the carpet.
7. Mr Brown goes to . . . office every day.
8. Tom, is this new car . . .?
9. Joe Stansbury is taking . . . pigs to market.
10. Mr Brown found . . . gloves in the car, but Mrs Brown
    left . . . at the post office.

J. *Put* who, whose *or* that *into these sentences:*
1. Susan gave some flowers to the girl . . . mother is ill.
2. Susan likes the girl . . . works at her office.
3. He took the pencil . . . was on that table.
4. He showed me the house . . . has a large garden.
5. We do not like people . . . do not like us.

K. *Put* some *or* any *into these sentences:*
1. There are . . . fine parks in London.
2. There aren't . . . houses on London Bridge now.
3. Did you see . . . boats on the river?
4. They have . . . friends in Switzerland.

5. I gave him . . . cigarettes, but I hadn't . . . matches.
6. Give your mother . . . of those flowers.
7. Are there . . . flowers in the sitting-room?
8. She isn't writing . . . letters today.
9. We haven't . . . oranges, but you can have . . . apples instead.
10. There were . . . cakes on that plate.

Cheap Seats

Young Bob does not like to spend money. But this evening he is taking a girl-friend to the cinema. They are at the box-office.

BOB: Two seats at twenty-five pence, please.

GIRL-FRIEND: I don't want to go in the twenty-five pence seats. They're too cheap.

BOB: All right. *One* seat at twenty-five pence, please.

LESSON 20

The Brown Family at Home

TONIGHT the Brown family are having an evening at home. Mr Brown, who was tired when he came home from the office, is sitting in an arm-chair, reading the evening paper which he has brought in with him. Mrs Brown is sitting by the fire making a woollen rug and watching the television. Susan was knitting, but now she has finished her knitting and she is watching the television, too. David is sitting at the table trying to do his homework, but he is not working very hard. The television is interesting, and he is watching it. The dog, Toby, is asleep by the fire. What a quiet family picture!

The Browns are a happy family. After their day's work they like to be at home together on one evening a week to talk, to play cards or to watch the television or listen to the radio.

Soon Susan and David will get up and go into the kitchen to make the supper. After the evening meal, Mrs Brown does not like to go into the kitchen again to make the supper. So Susan and David are going to make some tea or coffee and bring in some sandwiches or perhaps some cakes. Then, after the B.B.C. news, the Brown family will go to bed. They enjoy a pleasant evening at home.

CONVERSATION

MRS BROWN: Who's that man on the television now, Susan? I'm sure I've seen him somewhere.

SUSAN: Yes, I've seen him somewhere, too. Isn't he the man we saw at the theatre in London last week in that funny play?

MRS BROWN: The man whose tie fell into his soup?

SUSAN: Yes, I think he is. We'll ask David.

David, look at that man on the television. Isn't he the man in that play, *Summer Sunshine*, whose tie fell into his soup?

DAVID: Can't you see that I'm trying to do my homework? I haven't finished it yet. Yes, that's the man. I didn't think he was very funny.

MR BROWN: He's not very funny now. It's silly. Turn it off. Are we going to have a game of cards this evening?

MRS BROWN: What about David's homework? He hasn't done it yet.

MR BROWN: How long will you be, David?

DAVID: Five minutes. This is the last page.

SUSAN: Good. We haven't played cards for weeks. We'll bring the card-table near the fire; then we shan't get cold.

MRS BROWN: Susan, make a cup of coffee and some sandwiches while David is finishing his homework. There's some cold ham in the kitchen.

SUSAN: All right. Then David can wash up after the game.

MR BROWN (*he is reading the evening paper*): Do we know a Mr and Mrs Johnson in Orchard Road?

MRS BROWN: Isn't that the Johnson family whom we met at Bournemouth last summer? What's happened?

MR BROWN: She's had a baby.

DAVID: They were the people whose car broke down and we brought them back in ours.

MRS BROWN: Yes. They were nice people. They had one little boy. I didn't know she was going to have a baby. I'll write her a letter tomorrow. Perhaps I'll go to see her. Is it a boy or a girl? What have they called it?

MR BROWN: It's a boy. They've called it Andrew.

SUSAN (*coming in from the kitchen*): Here's the coffee.

MRS BROWN: Susan, Mrs Johnson's had a new baby. Was there enough milk?

SUSAN: For the baby or the coffee, Mother?

MRS BROWN: For the coffee, of course.

SUSAN: Yes, there was. I've left some for morning tea. Who's Mrs Johnson?

MRS BROWN: The people we brought back in the car from Bournemouth last summer.

SUSAN: Oh, I remember. How nice for her. Come on, David. Supper's ready.

DAVID: All right. I'm coming. I've finished my work.

MR BROWN: Good. Then we can play cards.

SENTENCE PATTERNS

58.   Present Perfect Tense—Regular Verbs

(See Grammar Summary 2, page 226)

Susan has finished her work at the office.
Mr Brown has carried the vegetables from the garden.
I have cooked the dinner.
We have walked from the station.
You have dropped a glass on the floor.
They have closed the doors and windows.

Has Susan picked any flowers for the sitting-room?
Has it rained today?
Have we smoked all the cigarettes?
Have you enjoyed your dinner?
Have they played cards this evening?
Who has opened the window?

Susan has not typed the letters yet.
Mr Brown has not worked in the garden today.
David has not washed his hands before dinner.
They have not cleaned their shoes.
We have not helped our friends.

59.   Present Perfect Tense—Irregular Verbs

(a) *Past Participle same as Past Tense*

Mrs Brown has told Susan to make the supper.
I have put the flowers in the dining-room.
We have stood here for two hours.
They have sold all the tickets for the theatre.
He has sat in his chair all the evening.
The sun has shone all the morning.

Has Mr Brown left his hat in the garden?
Have you spent all your money, David?
Has John found his books yet?
Have you read the paper this morning?

Mr Brown has not dug his garden this morning.
Mrs Brown has not bought any vegetables this week.
The baker has not brought any cakes today.
The clock has not struck five yet.

60. Present Perfect Tense—Irregular Verbs

(b) Past Participle different from Past Tense

David has gone to school this morning.
Tom has taken Susan to town in his car.
He has broken a window.
We have done our work.
The dog has eaten its dinner.
David has thrown the ball to the dog.

Has Mr Brown driven to the station this morning?
Have you given those letters to the postman?
Has Mrs Brown made a cake for tea?
Has Mr Robinson rung his bell yet?
Have you seen my brother this morning?

She has not sung to us this evening.
We have not shown him our garden.
I have not spoken to the boys this morning.
Susan and Tom have not swum in the water today.
They have not written to their friends in Switzerland.
David has not begun his homework yet.
He has not ridden a horse this summer.

61. Present Perfect Tense in Conversation

I have finished.	I've finished.	I haven't finished.
He has worked.	He's worked.	He hasn't worked.
She has asked.	She's asked.	She hasn't asked.
We have gone.	We've gone.	We haven't gone.
You have made.	You've made.	You haven't made.
They have sung.	They've sung.	They haven't sung.
John has spoken.	John's spoken.	John hasn't spoken.

NEW WORDS

arm-chair ('aːm'tʃeə)
card (kaːd)
  card-table ('kaːd teibl)
ham (ham)
knitting ('nitiŋ)
milk (milk)
news (njuːz)
page (peidʒ)
radio ('reidiou)
rug (rʌg)
soup (suːp)
television ('teli'viʒən)

Andrew ('andruː)
B.B.C. ('biːbiː'siː)
Bournemouth ('boːnməθ)
Johnson ('dʒonsn)

Orchard Road ('oːtʃəd 'roud)

happen, happened ('hapn, 'hapnd)
knit, knitted (nit, 'nitid)
remember, remembered (ri'membə, ri'membəd)
turn, turned (təːn, təːnd)

enough (i'nʌf)
pleasant ('pleznt)
silly ('sili)
sure ('ʃuə)
tonight (tə'nait)
woollen ('wulən)
yet (jet)

Idioms

how long will you be? ('hau 'loŋ wil juː 'biː)
how nice for her (hau 'nais fə həː)
I think he is (ai 'θiŋk hiː 'iz)
I'm sure I've seen him (aim 'ʃuə aiv 'siːn him)
she's had a baby (ʃiːz 'had ə 'beibi)
the car broke down (ðə 'kaː 'brouk 'daun)
they've called it Andrew (ðeiv 'koːld it 'andruː)
to get up (tə 'get 'ʌp)
to go to bed (tə 'gou tə 'bed)
to have an evening at home (tə 'hav ən 'iːvniŋ ət 'houm)
to make some tea (tə 'meik səm 'tiː)
on one evening a week (on 'wʌn 'iːvniŋ ə 'wiːk)
to play cards (tə 'plei 'kaːdz)
to wash up (tə 'woʃ 'ʌp)
to watch television (tə 'wotʃ teli'viʒən)
turn it off ('təːn it 'of)

we haven't played for weeks (wiː ˈhavnt ˈpleid fə ˈwiːks)
we shan't get cold (wiː ˈʃaɪnt get ˈkould)
what about . . .? (ˈwot əbaut)
what have they called it? (wot həv ðei ˈkoːld it)
what's happened? (ˈwots ˈhapnd)

EXERCISES

A. *Dictation*

Every week Mr and Mrs Brown and their children like to spend an evening together at home. This evening they have all finished their work and are sitting at home watching the television. They have eaten their dinner and David has done his homework. Now they are going to play cards. Mr Brown is reading the newspaper and his wife is making a rug; their daughter Susan is knitting. Now Susan is going to make some coffee in the kitchen. When Mrs Brown has finished cooking the evening meal for her family she doesn't like to go into the kitchen again to make the supper. Mr Brown has turned off the television, and for a moment the room is quiet.

B. *Answer these questions:*

1. What is Mr Brown reading?
2. Where has David been today?
3. Where is Susan going now?
4. What are the Browns going to do after supper?
5. Has David finished his homework yet?
6. Where did the Browns meet the Johnson family?
7. What have the Johnsons called their new baby?
8. What is Mrs Brown making?
9. Where is Susan going to put the card-table?
10. What do the Browns do when they spend an evening at home together?

C. *Put* who, whose, *or* which *into these sentences:*

1. The policeman wants to see the man . . . car is outside.
2. What is the name of the man . . . lives in the big house?

3. There are some people ... cannot be quiet in the theatre.
4. Are these the flowers ... came from your garden?
5. Is that the man ... goes to London with you each day?

D. *Put the verbs in these sentences into the Simple Past Tense:*

1. David is eating an apple.
2. Susan will go to the office.
3. Are you cooking the dinner?
4. Will Mr Brown drive to the station?
5. There are some people on the platform.
6. We know the man who sells cigarettes at the station.
7. Does Mr Brown live in that house?
8. Mrs Brown buys fruit from the greengrocer.
9. Tom will take Susan to the theatre.
10. The dog is running across the street.

E. *Put the verbs in these sentences into the Present Perfect Tense:*

1. Mrs Brown is writing to her friend.
2. Mr Brown will bring some vegetables from the garden.
3. He will take Susan to the seaside.
4. Susan is typing some letters for Mr Robinson.
5. Mrs Morton will buy some apples in the town.
6. Mr Robinson is not ringing the bell on his desk.
7. Mr Brown did not grow these flowers in his garden.
8. Will they swim to the little boat?
9. Are you speaking to those boys?
10. Will you throw that ball into the water?

F. *Finish these sentences:*

1. How much ... ?
2. How many ... ?
3. How long ... ?
4. How far ... ?
5. How old ... ?
6. Are there ... ?
7. Does he ... ?
8. Can you ... ?
9. Have they ... ?
10. Has he ... ?

G. *Put the right words into these sentences:*

1. David (*goes, is going*) to school every day.
2. Now we (*sit, are sitting*) in the class-room.
3. Dogs (*bark, are barking*) when they are hungry.
4. Susan (*goes, is going*) to the theatre this evening.
5. In this picture, Mrs Brown (*cooks, is cooking*) the Sunday dinner.
6. Mrs Brown (*buys, is buying*) all her bread from the baker.
7. It is eleven o'clock; I (*go, am going*) home now.
8. David (*finished, was finishing, has finished*) his work, and now he (*goes, is going*) to play football.
9. I (*wrote, was writing, have written*) a letter to my friend, and now I (*went, go, am going*) to post it.
10. Mrs Brown (*drove, was driving, has driven*) along the road when she (*heard, was hearing, has heard*) a dog barking.

H. *Put these words into sentences:*

1. I'm sure; 2. one evening a week; 3. not far from; 4. many years ago; 5. the other side of; 6. round the corner; 7. in front of; 8. stay at home; 9. look at; 10. after dinner.

I. *This paragraph tells step by step what Brian is doing. Rewrite this, saying what Brian has done.*

Brian is opening the classroom door; now he is closing the door again. He is walking across the room; he is going to the cupboard. Now he is taking a book from the cupboard. He is sitting down at his desk. He is starting to read his book. He is reading the first page. Now he is closing the book and is getting up from his desk. Now Brian is going home.

J. *Write about ten sentences on:* "An English Family at Home."

Still Not Perfect

A small schoolboy often wrote: 'I have went,' instead of 'I have gone'. At last his teacher said:

"You must stay after school this afternoon and write 'I have gone' a hundred times. Then you will remember it."

When the teacher came back he found a letter from the boy on his desk. It said:

Dear Sir,

I have wrote 'I have gone' a hundred times, and now I have went.

Jim Stone.

LESSON 21

A Picnic in the Country

A WEEK ago the Brown family went for a picnic in the country. It was early spring, so they thought it was too cold to go to the seaside. Mrs Brown packed a large basket of food and David put it in the back of the car. Susan's boy-friend, Tom Smith, went with them and one of David's friends from school whose name was Bob Sandford.

They set off early after breakfast, and drove about thirty

miles into the country until they came to their favourite place for picnicking. Here the fields slope gently south to a small stream, and a wood of tall trees keeps out the wind from the north and east. In the wood you can pick many spring flowers, and there are small fish in the stream.

In the picture we can see the Brown family and their friends having their picnic. They have left the car just inside the gate and David has carried the basket of food down through the fields to the edge of the stream. The sun is shining brightly and the ground is dry, so they can sit on the grass. They have found a pleasant place for their picnic. The young people have been into the wood to pick wild flowers, but Mr and Mrs Brown have sat quietly by the stream in the sunshine; Mrs Brown was reading a book and Mr Brown was fishing.

Now the young people have come back, and Mrs Brown has opened the basket and they are all having their tea. There are eggs, tomatoes, cheese rolls, lettuce sandwiches, cakes and fruit. There is tea in two large flasks.

At half past four they will put the plates, cups, saucers and other things back into the basket and they will go back to the car. They will get home at about half past five.

CONVERSATION

MRS BROWN: Well, you boys, you have been a long time, haven't you? Where've you been?

DAVID: Into the wood. I'm afraid we haven't picked any flowers, Mother. We climbed trees instead.

MRS BROWN: Have you torn your clothes? You always tear your clothes when you climb trees, don't you?

BOB: No, Mrs Brown, we haven't torn anything. We're a bit dirty, that's all.

MRS BROWN: Never mind. I can brush that off. Where's Susan?

DAVID: Haven't they come back yet? We lost them in the wood.

MRS BROWN: Here they are. Where have you two been?

SUSAN: We've been into the wood. We picked some wild flowers. Then we lost our way, didn't we, Tom? David, don't laugh.

DAVID: I'm not laughing.

SUSAN: Yes, you are. I'm hungry. Can we have tea now?

MRS BROWN: Yes. It's ready. Put the flowers under that tree, Susan. Now everyone, sit down on the grass.

BOB: Have you caught any fish, Mr Brown?

MR BROWN: Yes. One or two. But they're very small. I don't think there are many big fish in this stream.

DAVID: Where are the fish that you caught?

MR BROWN: They were very small. I threw them back into the water. You're laughing again, David, aren't you?

DAVID: Yes. You always throw the fish back. One day you'll catch a big one and keep it.

MRS BROWN: Then I shall put it into a glass case in the dining-room. Everyone will say: "Who caught that big fish?" and your father will smile and proudly say, "I did."

MR BROWN: Never mind. You like to laugh at me and pull my leg, don't you? But I like to fish. Sometimes I catch some fish, sometimes I don't, but I enjoy it.

TOM: Mr Brown is right. We can't work always. Everyone must play sometimes: David likes to play football, Bob likes to climb trees, Mr Brown likes to fish.

DAVID: And you and Susan like to pick wild flowers!

TOM: And you like to pull people's legs! Put another sandwich in his mouth, Mrs Brown, or I shall throw him into the stream.

SENTENCE PATTERNS

62.   Question-Tags—Positive

Sentences ending in a question-tag and asking for the answer,
'Yes'.

It is a nice day today, isn't it?
He is a tall boy, isn't he?
We are enjoying our holiday, aren't we?
You are a silly girl, aren't you?
They are busy this afternoon, aren't they?
You have a big house here, haven't you?
She has a lot of boy-friends, hasn't she?
He was the man you met at the theatre, wasn't he?
They were here last week, weren't they?

You and I are going to town tomorrow, aren't we?
He'll come with us to the seaside on Saturday, won't he?
We shall enjoy our day in the country, shan't we?
He was walking to the station when he met her, wasn't he?
The people were shouting and waving their arms, weren't they?
They have finished their homework now, haven't they?
She has left her handbag in the car, hasn't she?
She is talking to the greengrocer, isn't she?
The children are swimming in the water, aren't they?
You can swim as far as that boat, can't you?
They must go home now, mustn't they?
She lives in Bishopton, doesn't she?
Tom and Bob go to school together, don't they?
They go to London every day, don't they?
He bought a new car last week, didn't he?

63.   Question-Tags—Negative

Sentences ending in a question-tag and asking for the answer,
'No'.

It isn't raining now, is it?
David isn't at school today, is he?

You aren't hungry yet, are you?
You haven't a new car, have you?
She hasn't a brother still at school, has she?
They weren't at the theatre last night, were they?
He wasn't the man who bought your house, was he?

We aren't going to London on Monday, are we?
They aren't living in Birmingham now, are they?
That child won't fall into the water, will he?
We shan't catch the train, shall we?
He wasn't working all the morning, was he?
You weren't standing on the carpet with those dirty shoes, were
    you?
He hasn't taken my book from my room, has he?
They haven't sold their house in Bishopton, have they?
You can't eat all those cakes, can you?
The children mustn't go into the water when it's cold, must they?

He doesn't walk to the station every day, does he?
They don't swim when the water is cold, do they?
He didn't tear his coat, did he?
You didn't give her all the chocolates, did you?

NEW WORDS

case (keis)
east (iːst)
edge (edʒ)
fish (fiʃ)
flask (flaːsk)
ground (graund)
leg (leg)
lettuce ('letis)
north (noːθ)
roll (roul)
south (sauθ)
stream (striːm)

tomato (tə'maːtou)
wind (wind)
wood (wud)

Bob (bob)
Sandford ('sanfəd)

brush, brushed (brʌʃ, brʌʃt)
catch, caught (katʃ, koːt)
climb, climbed (klaim,
    klaimd)
keep, kept (kiːp, kept)
lose, lost (luːz, lost)

pack, packed (pak, pakt)
pull, pulled (pul, puld)
slope, sloped (sloup, sloupt)
tear, tore, torn (teə, tɔɪ, tɔɪn)

afraid (ə'freid)

brightly ('braitli)
dirty ('dəɪti)
favourite ('feivrit)
gently ('dʒentli)
proudly ('praudli)
wild (waild)

Idioms

I don't think there are . . . (ai 'dount 'θiŋk ðeə 'aɪ)
in the back of the car (in ðə 'bak əv ðə 'kaɪ)
just inside the gate ('dʒʌst in'said ðə 'geit)
one day you'll catch . . . ('wʌn 'dei juɪl 'katʃ)
that's all ('ðats 'ɔɪl)
to go for a picnic (tə 'gou fər ə 'piknik)
to keep out the wind (tə 'kiɪp aut ðə 'wind)
to pull his leg (tə 'pul hiz 'leg)
to set off (tə 'set 'of)
to sit under a tree (tə 'sit ʌndə ə 'triɪ)
we lost our way (wiɪ 'lost auə 'wei)
you have been a long time (juɪ 'hav bin ə 'loŋ 'taim)

EXERCISES

A. *Answer these questions:*

1. Where did the Browns go for their picnic?
2. What did Mrs Brown put in the basket?
3. Where did they leave the car?
4. What did David and Bob do in the wood?
5. What does Mr Brown like to do in the country?
6. What will Mrs Brown do when her husband catches a big fish?
7. How many people went to the picnic?
8. Who is Bob Sandford?
9. Did they go for their picnic in spring or summer?
10. At what time will they arrive home?

B. *Add the past participle to the verb in these sentences:*

David has . . . his homework.
David has *finished* his homework.

1. Mrs Brown has . . . the Sunday dinner.
2. He has . . . some oranges at the shop.
3. Tom has . . . Susan to the theatre.
4. Mr Brown has . . . the garden.
5. Susan has . . . a letter to her friend.
6. Mr Brown has . . . some fish in the stream.
7. Mrs Brown has . . . some food in a basket.
8. Have you . . . your hands this morning, David?
9. He has . . . ten cigarettes this morning.
10. Have you . . . the window, Bob?

C. *Write sentences with these question-tags at the end:*

1. . . ., isn't it?
2. . . ., weren't they?
3. . . ., hasn't she?
4. . . ., don't they?
5. . . ., didn't you?
6. . . ., aren't I?
7. . . ., can't they?
8. . . ., isn't he?
9. . . ., won't they?
10. . . ., shan't we?

D. *Write sentences with these question-tags at the end:*

1. . . ., am I?
2. . . ., are they?
3. . . ., was he?
4. . . ., had they?
5. . . ., did we?
6. . . ., can she?
7. . . ., will you?
8. . . ., shall we?
9. . . ., do they?
10. . . ., did she?

E. *Make these sentences negative:*

1. Tom was cleaning his new car.
2. Mr Brown caught some fish in the stream.
3. Mrs Brown is reading a book.
4. They will arrive home at six o'clock.
5. They have lost their way in the wood.
6. The teacher pointed to the map.
7. Susan goes to the office every day.
8. Mrs Brown likes to go to the shops in the morning.
9. The child is running across the street.
10. I have dropped my pen on the floor.

F. *Put these sentences into the interrogative:*

1. Mr Brown stood in front of the fire.
2. The dog has eaten its dinner.
3. Mrs Brown is reading a letter.
4. You have taken my book from the table.
5. Mr Brown drove his car to the station.
6. Schoolboys go to school on Saturdays.
7. They left the car just inside the gate.
8. David plays football every day.
9. We are learning English.
10. The people in the theatre were laughing.

G. *Change the verbs in these sentences into the Present Perfect Tense:*

1. Mr Brown is catching some fish.
2. Mrs Brown is brushing David's coat.
3. Bob is climbing a tall tree.
4. David and Bob are washing their hands.
5. The farmer is feeding the cows.
6. The actress is singing a song.
7. Mr Robinson is ringing the bell.
8. The van-driver is bringing some bread to our house.
9. The greengrocer is selling some oranges.
10. The boys are running across the road.

H. *Write ten sentences about* "The Countryside in Spring".

I. *Add a question-tag to these sentences:*

1. Susan hasn't written to her friend.
2. We didn't feed the chickens yesterday.
3. Susan, you haven't given David a cup of tea.
4. Mr Brown won't be in London tomorrow.
5. David doesn't go to school on Saturday.
6. They have sold all the cakes in the shop.
7. He'll drop that glass on the floor in a moment.
8. The farmer takes his pigs to market in a van.
9. Mr Brown must wash his hands before dinner.
10. Susan can swim very well.

J. *Put* who, whose *or* which *into these sentences:*

1. Is that the man . . . dog ran into our garden?
2. Children . . . run across the road are very silly.
3. Buckingham Palace is the house in . . . the Queen lives.
4. People . . . live in Bishopton go to London by train or by bus.
5. Mr Brown met a man . . . son goes to school with David.

K. *Put these verbs into sentences:*

catch; lose; break; clean; swim; speak; live; work; run; write.

L. *Make questions from the sentences you have written in* Exercise K.

Wrong Train

Oh, Mr Porter, whatever shall I do?
I wanted to go to Birmingham,
And you've taken me on to Crewe.
Take me back to London
As quickly as you can;
Oh, Mr Porter, what a *silly* girl I am!

Crewe (kruː)

LESSON 22

The Football Match

LAST Saturday afternoon David Brown and his father went to a football match at the Bishopton Football Ground. The Browns and many other Bishopton people think that theirs is the best team in the South of England. There were fifteen thousand people there. They came from far and near because it was the most important match of the year at Bishopton.

At three o'clock the two teams came on to the field. The Bishopton team (the 'home' team) were playing in blue and white shirts, the Easthampton City players (the visitors' team) were in red and white shirts.

The referee blew his whistle and the match began. For the first twenty minutes the Bishopton team were stronger and kept the ball in the Easthampton side of the field. Then, suddenly, an Easthampton player took the ball up the field and scored the first goal. The crowd shouted loudly. Soon after this, the referee blew the whistle because it was 'half-time'.

In the second half of the match the Bishopton team were again the better players. They tried hard, and after ten minutes they scored their first goal. They scored again after a quarter of an hour; then, before the last whistle blew, they scored a third goal and so won the match. All the Bishopton people in the crowd were very pleased, and went home happily to tea.

CONVERSATION

MR BROWN: Well, that was a good game. The best we've seen this winter.

DAVID: Yes. Better than last week. Easthampton have a good team, but the Bishopton players won because they're faster.

MR BROWN: Come on, David. The crowd's moving. We'll catch that bus. Then we can meet Mother in town for tea.

DAVID: Who are Bishopton playing next week?

MR BROWN: Cardiff City, I think.

DAVID: Do you think they'll win?

MR BROWN: I don't know. In Wales rugger is more important than soccer, but Cardiff have a good team this year.

DAVID: Which team will win the Cup?

MR BROWN: Blackpool have a good chance, but I think Manchester have a better.

DAVID: What about Bolton?

MR BROWN: They have, perhaps, the best chance of all.

DAVID: Why do you think so?

MR BROWN: Because they have a very fast team and some of their players are very clever with the ball; they can think as well as run, and that's the most important thing in football.

DAVID: Here's our bus. I think we shall get on.

MR BROWN: I hope so. Good, we're the last ones on. (*To the conductor*) Two into town, please.

BUS CONDUCTOR: Six pence, please. Three pence each. Ten pence. Four pence change. Fares, please. Have your fares ready, please.

DAVID: Can you get tickets for the Cup this year?

MR BROWN: Yes, I think so. Mr Brook knows the secretary of the Bishopton Football Club. He's said he'll get me two tickets.

DAVID: Can you get three? Tom Smith wants to go.

MR BROWN: I'll try. But it's harder every year to get tickets, because so many people want to go. And they'll be more expensive this year. Here's our stop. We get off here. There's your mother, waiting to go for tea.

SENTENCE PATTERNS

64. Comparison of Adjectives

(*a*) *-er, -est*

David is a fast runner.
Bob is a faster runner than David.
Jones is the fastest runner in the school.

It is cold in winter.
Winter is colder than summer.
January is the coldest month in the year.

This is a hard exercise.

Exercise A is harder than Exercise B.
This is the hardest lesson in the book.

Susan is a pretty girl.
Susan is prettier than Joan.
Mary is the prettiest girl in the office.

This is a busy street.
The London streets are busier than the streets in Bishopton.
Oxford Street is one of the busiest streets in London.

David thought the lesson was easy.
Exercise B is easier than Exercise A.
Lesson 1 is the easiest in the book.

Mr Brown was not hungry.
David was hungrier than his father.
David was the hungriest person in the family.

David is a tall boy.
Tom is taller than David.
Bob is the tallest boy in the class.

This is a big house.
Our house is bigger than yours.
He has the biggest house in Bishopton.

Mr Brook is fat.
He is fatter than Mr Brown.
He was the fattest man in the room.

The sun is hot today.
Summer is hotter than winter.
July is the hottest month of the year.

Mr Brown is a thin man.
He is thinner than his friend Mr Brook.
He was not the thinnest man in the office.

John is a good footballer.
Bob is a better footballer than John.
Tom is the best footballer in the school.

(b) More, Most

The postman brought an important letter.
This letter is more important than that.
He is the most important man in the office.

They have a beautiful garden.
Their garden is more beautiful than ours.
This is the most beautiful garden in Bishopton.

I have read an interesting book.
This book is more interesting than that.
This is the most interesting book I have read.

She bought an expensive coat.
This hat is more expensive than the one in the window.
She wanted the most expensive hat in the shop.

65.   Why? Because

Why did Mr Brown take a bus into Bishopton?
Because he wanted to meet Mrs Brown for tea.
Why did the Bishopton team win?
Because they were the faster players.
Why did the crowd shout loudly?
Because they were pleased.
Why were they pleased?
Because their team won the match.
Why does the referee blow his whistle?
Because someone has scored a goal.
Why isn't Mr Brown eating his breakfast?
Because he isn't hungry.
Why did Mrs Brown go to town?
Because she wanted to buy some fruit and vegetables.
Why is David going to clean his shoes?
Because they are dirty.
Why do people go to the football ground?
Because they want to see the match.

Why have you left your breakfast on the table?
Because I'm not hungry this morning.
Why aren't you at school this morning, David?
Because I'm not well today.

66.   Reason Clauses—*Because*

He went to bed because he was tired.
They won the match because they were the better team.
You must hurry because you are late.
We didn't go to London because we missed the train.
Susan was smiling because she was happy.
We will have salad for lunch because John likes it.
Did you go home because you weren't well?
We can't come tomorrow because we are going into the country.
He lives in London because he works there.
You must put your coat on because it's cold.

NEW WORDS

chance (tʃaːns)
club (klʌb)
conductor (kənˈdʌktə)
crowd (kraud)
fare (feə)
goal (goul)
player (ˈpleiə)
referee (ˈrefəˈriː)
rugger (Rugby football) (ˈrʌgə, ˈrʌgbi ˈfutbɔːl)
soccer (Association football) (ˈsokə, əˈsousiˈeiʃn ˈfutbɔːl)
stop (stop)
team (tiːm)
whistle (ˈwisl)
Blackpool (ˈblakpuːl)

Bolton (ˈboultən)
Easthampton (ˈiːstˈhamtən)

blow, blew, blown (blou, bluː, bloun)
hope, hoped (houp, houpd)
move, moved (muːv, muːvd)
score, scored (skɔː, skɔːd)
win, won (win, wʌn)

because (biˈkoz)
best (best)
better (ˈbetə)
clever (ˈklevə)
happily (ˈhapili)
more (mɔː)

other ('ʌðə)   than (ðən)
strong (strɔŋ)   why (wai)

Idioms

fares, please! ('feəz 'pliːz)
from far and near (frəm 'faː ənd 'niə)
half-time ('haːf 'taim)
I hope so (ai 'houp sou)
to catch a bus (tə 'katʃ ə 'bʌs)
we get off here (wiː 'get 'of 'hiə)

EXERCISES

A. *Dictation*

In England many people like to go to football matches.
Every Saturday afternoon in winter thousands of people
crowd into the football grounds to watch their favourite teams
play. The games begin at three o'clock and finish at about a
quarter to five. Sometimes in the spring, when the days are
longer, the matches are in the evening. Football began in
England, but now many people in other countries play the
game. Every year there are matches between one country and
another to see which country has the better team.

B. *Answer these questions in sentences:*

1. When are football matches played in England?
2. At what time did this match start?
3. What was the colour of the shirts which the Bishopton
   team wore?
4. Which was the better team?
5. When did the Easthampton team get their first goal?
6. When did the Bishopton team score their first goal?

7. Who does Mr Brown think will win the Cup?
8. How much did Mr Brown pay for their bus fare?
9. Whom will Mr Brown ask for tickets for the Cup match?
10. Why does Mr Brown think that Bolton will win the Cup?

C. *Put these adjectives into sentences different from those in the Sentence Patterns:*

good; faster; harder; best; tallest; better; small; prettiest; busier; bigger.

D. *Finish these sentences:*

1. Mr Brown likes ...
2. David wants ...
3. Tom can ...
4. Susan must ...
5. Mrs Brown will ...
6. The baker doesn't ...
7. The teacher won't ...
8. We shan't ...
9. Can they ...?
10. Must he ...?
11. Do they want ...?
12. Does she like ...?

E. *Give the questions to which these are the answers:*

1. Because she likes shopping.
2. Because they wanted to meet Mrs Brown for tea.
3. Because it is Saturday today.
4. Because Susan was late at the office this morning.
5. Because the sea is too cold.
6. Because the bus is full.
7. Because it is five o'clock.
8. Because he has bought a new car.
9. Because she is very busy at home this morning.
10. Because he is not well.

F. *Put the right word into these sentences:*

1. David is (*tall, taller, tallest*) than Susan.
2. Mr Brown is not (*hungry, hungrier, hungriest*) this morning.
3. Bob is a (*good, better, best*) footballer than David.
4. These people have the (*large, larger, largest*) house in Bishopton.
5. Tom has bought a very (*fast, faster, fastest*) car.
6. Lesson 1 is (*easy, easier, easiest*) than Lesson 2.
7. Today is the (*cold, colder, coldest*) day we have had this year.
8. On Sunday morning Mrs Brown is the (*busy, busier, busiest*) person in the house.
9. Joan is a (*pretty, prettier, prettiest*) girl, but Susan is (*pretty, prettier, prettiest*).
10. When Tom bought his new car, he was the (*happy, happier, happiest*) man in Bishopton.

G. *Write these in words:*

(*a*) 45; 28; 19; 22; 40.
(*b*) 6.15 P.M.; 3.30 A.M.; 5.40 P.M.; 2.10 A.M.; 11.50 P.M.

H. *Put the possessive adjective or pronoun into these sentences:*

1. The girl is talking to . . . friend.
2. I have lost . . . book.
3. Is this . . . new car, Tom?
4. The Bishopton players scored . . . first goal.
5. I have found . . . pen; have you found . . . ?
6. We left . . . car just inside the gate.
7. The dog was eating . . . dinner.
8. David has finished . . . exercise, so he is helping me with . . .
9. David and Susan are going to Switzerland for . . . holiday this year.
10. I have finished . . . work, but Susan hasn't finished . . .

I. *Put these prepositions into sentences, one sentence for each:*
between; off; above; beside; across; with; after; through; near; down.

J. *Put the right verb into these sentences:*
1. We have (*buy*) a new house in London.
2. They have (*catch*) the bus.
3. Yesterday David (*find*) five pence in the street.
4. He has (*do*) all his homework.
5. I have (*leave*) my car near the gate.
6. She has (*sing*) three songs to her friends.
7. The sun (*shine*) all day yesterday.
8. They have (*come*) to the house to meet David.
9. We (*send*) a letter to our friends in Switzerland last week.
10. The greengrocer has (*sell*) all his oranges.

K. *Add a noun to the verbs in these sentences:*
1. Mrs Brown saw . . . in the sky.
2. Susan wrote . . . to her friend yesterday.
3. The Browns have . . . in their garden.
4. Mr Brown drove . . . to the station.
5. Tom took . . . to London yesterday.
6. Mrs Brown is cooking . . .
7. You will find . . . on the table in the dining-room.
8. Your glass is empty; will you have . . .
9. David did not play . . . last Saturday.
10. Close . . ., please, David.

L. *Put these words into sentences, with the verbs in the Present Perfect Tense:*
1. David—do—homework.
2. Susan—go—theatre.
3. Mr Brown—catch—fish.
4. Mrs Brown—buy—vegetables.
5. Mr Brook—sell—house.
6. Bob—meet—friend.
7. The boy—find—five pence.

8. The girl—write—mother.
9. Mr Robinson—ring—bell.
10. Tom—drive—new car.

M. *Write a composition about the Brown family.*

N. *Write a composition about the things in England which are different from those in your country.*

Asking Too Much

Here is another story about an Irishman.

An Englishman was driving along a country road in Ireland and met a man carrying a heavy bag.

"Can I take you into town?" the Englishman asked.

The Irishman said "Thank you," and got into the car.

In a few minutes the driver saw that the Irishman was sitting with the heavy bag still in his hand.

"Why don't you put your bag down?" he asked.

"Well," answered the Irishman, "you've given me a ride in your car. I can't ask you to carry my bag as well."

Ireland (ˈaiələnd)
heavy (ˈhevi)
Englishman (ˈiŋgliʃmən)

LESSON 23

Getting Ready for Christmas

IT will soon be Christmas. Mrs Brown has bought some presents for the family and their friends. She hopes to get all her presents early this year. When Christmas is near you can't buy anything nice in the shops; you can only get things you don't want.

Mr Brown has a cousin, Tony Mason. Tony and his wife Brenda are much younger than Mr and Mrs Brown, but a little older than Susan and David. They have two small children. The Browns often invite the Masons to spend Christmas with them, and they are going to do so again this year. The Masons live in Scotland, so the Browns have not seen them since last Christmas. Susan's boy-friend Tom will be there, too, so it will be a gay party.

Susan has written to Tony and Brenda, inviting them for Christmas. Here is the letter she wrote:

Oak Tree House,
Felton Road,
Bishopton,
Surrey.
3rd December, 19—

Dear Brenda and Tony,

What are you doing for Christmas? The family will be very pleased to have you and the children here with us again this year. Tom Smith—you met him last year—will be here, so we shall have as gay a time as we usually have at Christmas.

We have a new television-set—the very latest—and Father has already booked seats for the pantomime. We shall have a big party on one evening. David and I have bought a lot of the latest dance records, so we can have some dancing at the party. The children will be all right. As you know, we have plenty of room and they can have their presents from the Christmas tree, as they do at home. You will come, won't you?

Mother and Father send their love. David says he's sorry he hasn't written to you, but he's been very busy at school. He wants to go up to Oxford next October and must work hard.

Yours with love,
Susan

When Tony and Brenda Mason get Susan's letter they will be very pleased. They always enjoy going to stay with the Browns at Bishopton, and their children, Jackie and Sheila, enjoy it too. The Browns are always glad to see them. The Browns and their cousins the Masons have always been good friends, and Christmas is a happy time that everyone ought to enjoy. In England, the most important day is Christmas Day and not Christmas Eve. On Christmas Day people give presents to their family and friends, and have their Christmas dinner.

CONVERSATION

SUSAN: What are we doing for Christmas, Mother?

MRS BROWN: What do you want to do?

SUSAN: We can have some people to stay with us, can't we?

MRS BROWN: Yes, I think so. Who do you want?

SUSAN: Tony and Brenda and their children. They're very nice, aren't they? And we haven't seen them since last Christmas.

MRS BROWN: All right, then. I'm always glad to see Brenda and Tony. Do you want Father to get tickets for the pantomime?

SUSAN: Oh, yes. Children always enjoy the pantomime, don't they?

MRS BROWN: And a lot of people who're not children enjoy it, too. We must get a big Christmas tree and put all the presents on the tree. Where will they sleep?

SUSAN: Oh, we've plenty of room, haven't we? The children can have my room, Tony can go in with David, and Brenda and I'll have the guest-room.

(*David comes in*)

SUSAN: Oh, David, Mother's going to invite Tony and Brenda for Christmas.

DAVID: Good. Are we going to have a party, too? I want to play my new dance records.

SUSAN: Yes, we'll roll up the carpets and open the doors between the sitting-room and dining-room as we always do at Christmas. That'll give us plenty of room for dancing, won't it?

MRS BROWN: Have you two bought your Christmas presents yet?

SUSAN: I've already bought some of mine. You haven't bought any, David, have you?

DAVID: Well, no. Last week I spent all my money on dance records, and I haven't had any money since then; but I shall have some more between now and Christmas.

MRS BROWN: Who is going to write to Tom and Brenda?

SUSAN ⎫ David!
DAVID ⎭ Susan!

DAVID: I'm too busy. If I want to go up to Oxford next October I must work hard at school. I've no time for writing letters. You ought to write, Susan.

MRS BROWN: Have you written to them since the summer?

SUSAN: No, I'm afraid not. All right, I'll write to them. Is there anything else?

MRS. BROWN: No, I don't think so. I'll do all the shopping. I think we shall have a very nice Christmas.

SENTENCE PATTERNS

67.   *Ought*

You ought to go home now, children.

David ought to work hard at school.

You ought to write to your cousins.

Mr Brown ought to change his shoes when he comes in from the garden.

You ought to take some flowers to your mother, Susan.

Mr Brook ought to wear a coat on cold mornings.

Children ought to go to bed early when they are young.

You ought not to drive so fast through the town.

Susan ought not to come late to the office.

You ought not to run across the street in front of a car.

They ought not to swim in the sea when the water is cold.
People ought not to walk on the carpet in dirty shoes.

Ought you to be in bed now, David?
Ought I to swim in that cold water?
Ought he to jump on the train when it's moving?
Ought Tom to drive so fast through the town?
Ought they to come to school so late every morning?

68.   Position of Adverbs

(See Sentence Pattern 78, page 215)

He does his work well.
He spoke to her quietly.
He drives his car carefully.
She wanted to do her shopping quickly.
They will arrive here tomorrow.
He came to see me yesterday.
The train stopped suddenly.
I shall meet her in town today.
She answered him slowly.

69.   *So*

Is he going to London tomorrow?	I think so.
Are they at the theatre this evening?	I think so.
Has David gone home?	Yes, I think so.
Will it rain today?	Yes, I think so.
Have the Browns sold their house yet?	Yes, I think so.
Do the Brooks live in Bishopton?	Yes, I think so.
Is that your coat?	No, I don't think so.
Are you going to the theatre this evening?	No, I don't think so.
Has David finished his work yet?	No, I don't think so.
Did Tom buy a new car?	No, I don't think so.
Can Susan swim very well?	No, I don't think so.
Will David play football on Saturday?	No, I don't think so.
Are you going to the seaside tomorrow?	Yes, I hope so.
Have they any eggs at the farm?	I hope so.

Is Tom going to take you to the theatre?	Yes, I hope so.
Has David found his pen?	I hope so.
Does Mr Robinson want these letters before lunch?	Yes, he said so.
Did Tom and Susan enjoy the play?	Yes, they said so.
Is Mr Brown going to London tomorrow?	He didn't say so.
Did he meet Tom in London?	He didn't say so.

70.   *Since*

I have been here since last October.

David has been in bed since Tuesday.

I have been to Cardiff since I saw you last week.

We have lived in this house since last February.

Have you been here since one o'clock?   Yes, I have.

Have you seen Tom since Monday?

> Yes, I saw him on Wednesday.

Have you been to London since you came to this country?

How long have you been in England?

> I have been here since October (*or* Since October).

Mr Brown hasn't been to London since last Friday.

They haven't been here since Christmas.

I haven't seen her since last summer.

It hasn't rained since the Thursday of last week.

NEW WORDS

cousin ('kʌzn)	Christmas Eve ('krisməs 'iːv)
dance (daːns)	Felton ('feltn)
dancing ('daːnsiŋ)	Jackie ('dʒaki)
guest-room ('gestrum)	Oak Tree House ('ouk triː 'haus)
love (lʌv)	Oxford ('oksfəd)
pantomime ('pantəmaim)	Sheila ('fiːlə)
party ('parti)	Surrey ('sʌri)
present ('preznt)	Tony Mason ('touni 'meisn)
record ('rekoːd)	
	invite, invited (in'vait,
Brenda ('brendə)	in'vaitid)

ought (ɔɪt)
roll, rolled (roul, rould)
sleep, slept (sliːp, slept)

already (ɔɪl'redi)
else (els)

glad (glad)
if (if)
latest ('leitist)
plenty ('plenti)
since (sins)

Idioms

as you know ('az juɪ 'nou)
I'm afraid not (aim ə'freid 'not)
I'm glad to see them (aim 'glad tə 'siː ðəm)
is there anything else? (iz ðeə 'eniθiŋ 'els)
it will soon be Christmas (it wil 'suːn bi 'krisməs)
mother sends her love ('mʌðə 'sendz həɪ 'lʌv)
plenty of room ('plenti əv 'ruːm)
the very latest (ðə 'veri 'leitist)
to go up to Oxford (tə 'gou ʌp tə 'oksfəd)
to have no time for (tə hav 'nou 'taim fə)
to roll up the carpet (tə 'roul 'ʌp ðə 'kaɪpit)
yours with love ('jɔɪz wið 'lʌv)

EXERCISES

A. *Answer these questions:*

1. Why does Mrs Brown buy her Christmas presents early?
2. How many children have Tony and Brenda Mason, and what are their names?
3. Who will visit the Browns at Christmas as well as the Mason family?
4. When did Susan write to the Masons?
5. Why didn't David write the letter?
6. Why hadn't David any money to buy presents?
7. Where will the Browns put their Christmas presents on Christmas Day?
8. Why did David want a party?
9. In what month does Christmas come?
10. Why do children enjoy Christmas?

B. *Add question-tags to these sentences:*

1. He is in London today, . . .?
2. You are Susan's brother, . . .?
3. The Browns are a happy family, . . .?
4. I am good at English, . . .?
5. He has a book in his hand, . . .?
6. They were at the theatre last night, . . .?
7. I can have these cakes for my tea, . . .?
8. You will write to him next week, . . .?
9. They did their homework before they went out, . . .?
10. He works hard at school, . . .?

C. *Add question-tags to these sentences:*

1. He isn't in this room, . . .?
3. You aren't going to town today, . . .?
3. He hasn't lost his pen, . . .?
4. You don't live with the Browns, . . .?
5. You won't eat all the chocolates, . . .?
6. He can't come with us tomorrow, . . .?
7. She didn't go to the theatre yesterday, . . .?
8. They haven't finished their work, . . .?
9. We shan't lose our train, . . .?
10. She wasn't late at the office this morning, . . .?

D. *Write sentences to which these can be the answers:*

1. I think so.
2. We hope so.
3. They said so.
4. No, I don't think so.
5. Yes, I think so.
6. Yes, we hope so.
7. Yes, he said so.
8. We think so.
9. They hope so.
10. He hopes so.

E. *Make these sentences negative:*

1. There are some apples on that tree.
2. Their friends will arrive before eight o'clock.
3. The postman brought some letters this morning.
4. David cleaned his father's car yesterday.

5. Mrs Brown often drives the car.
6. Children enjoy a day at the seaside.
7. I saw the child fall into the water.
8. Mr Brown grows vegetables in his garden.
9. Susan helped her mother in the kitchen.
10. David knows the postman's name.

F. *Write a letter from Brenda Mason to Susan, saying that they will be pleased to spend Christmas with the Browns.*

G. *Put these phrases into sentences:*

as well as; many years ago; all the same; at once; at first; not very far from; at the moment; to look after; a lot of; at the end of.

H. *Add an adjective to each of these sentences:*

1. Susan is a . . . girl.
2. David is a . . . boy.
3. I have read a . . . book.
4. She picked some . . . and . . . flowers.
5. The train was . . .
6. The bus was . . ., so we waited for the next.
7. This . . . boy had the right answers to all the teacher's questions.
8. The Browns have a . . . garden round their house.
9. Tom has bought a . . . car.
10. Mr Brown didn't eat his breakfast because he wasn't . . .

I. *Put these words into sentences, using the Simple Past Tense:*

1. Susan—write—letter.
2. David—go—football match.
3. Children—climb—trees.
4. Mrs Brown—buy—bread.
5. Mr Brook—find—money.
6. The policeman—stop—cars.
7. The dog—eat—dinner.
8. The cricketer—throw—ball.

9. David—break—window.
10. The boy—lose—his pencil.

J. *Put an adverb into each of these sentences:*

1. Mr Brown was in London . . ., but he is at home today.
2. When a play has started, people walk . . . into the theatre.
3. You must not drive . . . in a crowded street.
4. The train came . . . into the station.
5. He was . . ., but I don't know where he is . . .
6. Don't go . . ., he will be here . . .
7. The Brown family live . . . together.
8. The sun was shining . . .
9. When Tom spoke . . ., Susan told him to be quiet.
10. She ran . . . to find the doctor.

K. *Write two short answers to each of these questions:*

Is David at home today?   Yes, he is.
                               No, he isn't.

1. Will it soon be Christmas?
2. Has David bought his Christmas presents?
3. Did Bishopton win their football match against Easthampton?
4. Has Mr Brown cut the grass yet?
5. Can Susan cook the Sunday dinner?
6. Does Tom like driving a car?
7. Are the Browns a happy family?
8. Have the Masons been to Bishopton before?
9. Were Susan and Tom in London yesterday?
10. Will the Masons be pleased to spend Christmas with the
    Browns?

L. *Finish these sentences:*

1. The schoolboys are pleased when . . .
2. I have read the letter which . . .
3. Do you know the man who . . . ?
4. They had dinner before . . .
5. That is the boy whom . . .

6. We are looking for the girl to whom ...
7. I was speaking to the woman whose ...
8. Have you seen the book which ...
9. Our friends arrived while ...
10. She doesn't know where ...

M. *Write a composition about the Browns' house at Bishopton.*
(There are pictures on pages 57, 64, 135 and 170.)

N. *Write a composition about English food. How is it different from the food in your country?*

Nothing to be Cross About

Jack had two apples and gave the smaller one to his little brother Fred.

"You are rude, Jack," said Fred.

"Why?" asked Jack.

"Because you've given me the smaller apple. If I have two apples, I'm polite; I always give the larger one away and keep the smaller one."

"Well, why are you cross?" asked Jack. "You've got the smaller one, haven't you?"

cross (kros)
rude (ruːd)

LESSON 24

Christmas Day

CHRISTMAS has come at last. Tony and Brenda Mason and their two small children, Jackie and Sheila, arrived about tea-time on Christmas Eve, and after a good meal the children went off to bed. They were very excited, and before bedtime they called up the chimney to Father Christmas and told him what they wanted; then they hung up their stockings at the foot of their beds. Jackie wanted to hang up a pillow-case, but Sheila told him that was greedy. Now they are both fast asleep.

The house is looking really beautiful. All this last week, Mrs Brown and the woman who comes to help her with the housework worked hard cleaning and getting the house ready for the visitors. The day before Christmas Eve was Sunday, so Mr Brown and David were working all day putting up the holly and coloured paper over the doors and pictures. They put a big Christmas tree just inside the front door, and hung coloured electric lights among the branches. Everything looks very gay and exciting.

Christmas is a time of joy and happiness. People forget sadness and try to show kindness to everyone. Children look forward to Christmas for many weeks. The warmth and friendship of Christmas help us to forget the darkness and cold of winter.

When the children wake up on Christmas morning their presents will be beside their beds and they will think that Father Christmas has brought them. During the morning, Mrs Brown and Brenda will cook the Christmas dinner. Mr Brown, Tony and the children will go to church. The church is always very crowded on Christmas morning. For Christmas dinner they will have turkey and Christmas pudding. In the afternoon they will see and hear the Queen on television; then the older people will rest while the children play games. In England most people spend Christmas Day at home with their families.

CONVERSATION

JACKIE MASON (*waking up in the early hours of the morning*):
Wake up, Sheila. He's come! Father Christmas has come!

SHEILA: He's brought me such a lot of presents. I've got a doll and a doll's house, and three books and some coloured pencils and a lot of other things. What have you got?

JACKIE: I've got a new football and a box of soldiers and some books.

SHEILA: What's in your stocking?

JACKIE: Some sweets and an orange and an apple and a six-pence and lots of other things.

SHEILA: Shall we get up now?

JACKIE: No, we'll stay in bed until morning and play with our toys.

• • • • •

MRS BROWN: Wake up, everyone. It's Christmas morning. Who's going to church this morning?

MR BROWN: Tony and I will take David, Susan and the children, if you and Brenda will cook the dinner.

MRS BROWN: All right. Then we can have some games for the children this afternoon, after we've seen the Queen.

BRENDA: Doesn't the Christmas tree look nice? You've done it very well this year.

SUSAN: There's a present on it for everyone. David and I put them on yesterday. We'll have the presents from the tree after tea.

MR BROWN: Hurry up. If we don't hurry, we'll be late for church. The bells are ringing.

• • • • •

BRENDA (*after tea*): Now children, Father Christmas has brought you a lot of presents, and you've had another one from the tree, and now it's time for bed.

SHEILA: What a nice Christmas. I shall take my new doll to bed with me.

JACKIE: I think I've eaten too much.

TONY: You'll be all right in the morning, if you go to sleep at once. And tomorrow we're going to the pantomime.

JACKIE: Oh, good! Can I sit next to David? He always makes me laugh.

BRENDA: Yes, if you want to. Now, come on, up to bed!

. . . . .

MRS BROWN: Oh dear! I'm so tired.

MR BROWN: The children have enjoyed it. And Christmas is the children's day. We'll have a drink and then a game of cards.

SUSAN: Sit down by the fire, Mother. You must be tired. David and I'll make the supper.

TONY: And Brenda and I will do the washing up.

SENTENCE PATTERNS

71.   Condition Clauses—*If*

You can do well if you work hard.
We go to bed if we are tired.
He has an egg for breakfast if there isn't any bacon.
He likes to swim in the sea if the water is warm.
We always go shopping on Monday if it isn't raining.
You can hear the birds singing if you listen.
She must go home if she isn't well.
You can stay to dinner if you like.
The crowd is happy if their team scores a goal.
Tom enjoys the theatre if the play is good.

We shall go to the seaside tomorrow if it is fine.
He will stay in bed if he is ill.
They will swim in the sea if the sun is shining.
I will drive you to the station if you like.
I am going to bed now if you don't mind.
I am going to the theatre this evening if there is a good play.

I am coming home early this evening if I can.
They are going to the pantomime if they are good children.

72.   Position of Frequency Adverbs
                (See Sentence Pattern 68, page 204)

He always plays football on Saturday.
They often spend Christmas at Bishopton.
Susan sometimes arrives late at the office.
They usually go to Scotland for their holidays.
He never works on Saturday afternoons.

Does he always play football on Saturday?
Do they often spend Christmas at Bishopton?
Does Susan sometimes arrive late at the office?
Do they usually go to Scotland for their holidays?
Does he ever work on Saturday afternoons?

I have always wanted to go to Switzerland.
We have often seen her in the town.
They have usually finished their work by tea-time.
He has never been to this house.

Have you always wanted to go to Switzerland?
Has she often been here?
Have they usually finished their work by tea-time?
Has he ever been to this house?

73.   Preposition at End of Sentence

Who are you speaking to?
Where did you get that book from?
Who is that present for?
Who did you go with?
Who is that book by?
What did you carry it in?
What did you do that for?

What are you looking at?
What are you looking for?
Whose car has she gone in?
Which chair is the dog sitting under?
Which train did you come by?
What's he talking about?
Which shop has she gone into?
Which gate did he climb over?
This is the man he was telling you of.
He was the man I was sitting next to.
Are those the stairs she fell down?

74.   *Do*

He is doing his homework.
She does her housework in the morning.
She does her shopping in the afternoon.
She does the cooking every Sunday.
He does the garden on Saturday afternoon.
He has done the painting very well.
Have you done my letters, Miss Brown?
Has he done any fishing this summer?
I never do any swimming when it's cold.
He doesn't do much walking; he always goes by car.
She sat quietly by the fire, doing her knitting.

75.   *For*
(See Sentence Pattern 70, page 205 for *Since*)

Past Time
He has been here for a week.
I haven't been to London for five years.
He waited for a whole hour.

Future Time
How long are you here for?
I am here for a year.
I shall stay in England for a month.

NEW WORDS

branch (braɪntʃ)
chimney ('tʃimni)
darkness ('daɪknis)
doll (dol)
drink (driŋk)
friendship ('frendʃip)
happiness ('hapinis)
holly ('holi)
joy (dʒoi)
kindness ('kaindnis)
pillow-case ('piloukeis)
pudding ('pudiŋ)
sadness ('sadnis)
stocking ('stokiŋ)

sweet (swiːt)
turkey ('təːki)
warmth (woːmθ)
washing-up ('woʃiŋ 'ʌp)

hang, hung (haŋ, hʌŋ)
rest, rested (rest, 'restid)

ever ('evə)
excited (iks'aitid)
forward ('foːwəd)
greedy ('griːdi)
over ('ouvə)
usually ('juːʒuəli)

Idioms

at the foot of the bed (ət ðə 'fut əv ðə 'bed)
doesn't it look nice? ('dʌznt it luk 'nais)
during the morning ('djuəriŋ ðə 'moːniŋ)
fast asleep ('faːst ə'sliːp)
he makes me laugh (hiː 'meiks miː 'laːf)
in the early hours of the morning (in ði 'əːli 'auəz əv ðə 'moːniŋ)
it's time for bed (its 'taim fə 'bed)
such a lot of ('sʌtʃ ə 'lot əv)
the house is looking beautiful (ðə 'haus iz 'lukiŋ 'bjuːtiful)
they went off to bed (ðei 'went of tə 'bed)
to get into bed (tə 'get intə 'bed)
to have a drink (tə 'hav ə 'driŋk)
to look forward to (tə 'luk 'foːwəd tə)
you must be tired (juː 'mʌst bi 'taiəd)

EXERCISES

A. *Answer these questions:*

1. On which day does Christmas come?
2. How many people spent Christmas in the Browns' house?
3. What are the names of the Mason children?
4. What did the children do on Christmas Eve before they went to bed?
5. Why do English people enjoy Christmas?
6. Who did the Browns listen to on the afternoon of Christmas Day?
7. How often each year does Christmas come?
8. What did the Browns have for their Christmas dinner?
9. What is the difference between radio and television?
10. What do English people go to see in the theatre at Christmas?

B. *Write about Christmas (or some other holiday) in your own country.*

C. *Put the right adjective into these sentences:*

1. Bob is the . . . footballer in his school. (*good*)
2. Susan's hat was . . . than her mother's. (*expensive*)
3. I have read a very . . . book (*interesting*)
4. This is the . . . exercise in the book. (*hard*)
5. I think Susan is much . . . than Joan. (*pretty*)
6. Tom is a . . . swimmer than Susan. (*good*)
7. This was the . . . day in his life. (*important*)
8. They went to London in a . . . train. (*slow*)
9. This exercise is . . . than the last one. (*easy*)
10. Which is the . . . city in England? (*beautiful*)

D. *Put the adverb into the right place in these sentences:*

1. I go to the theatre in the evening. (*often*)
2. Mrs Brown goes shopping on Monday. (*usually*)
3. Have you lived on a farm? (*ever*)
4. I have an egg for my breakfast. (*always*)

5. We like to go to the seaside on Saturday. (*sometimes*)
6. Mr and Mrs Brown have lived in London. (*never*)
7. Have you been shopping in Bishopton? (*often*)
8. She does not drink coffee in the morning. (*usually*)
9. Do you travel to London by train? (*always*)
10. We don't go to Switzerland for our holidays. (*often*)

E. *Finish these sentences:*

1. If you go to London, ...
2. If he has lost his pen, ...
3. If Susan is late at the office, ...
4. If Mr Brown is not well, ...
5. If David works hard, ...
6. If the dinner is ready, ...
7. If you go to town this afternoon, ...
8. If Mr Brown catches small fish, ...
9. If she sees a coat she likes, ...
10. If we don't hurry, ...

F. *Put a preposition into each of these sentences:*

1. What are you thinking . . .?
2. Is there any difference . . . grass and hay?
3. They have a nice garden . . . their house.
4. Where did you get those flowers . . .?
5. They had tea in town . . . the football match.
6. She walked slowly . . . the room.
7. David jumped . . . the water.
8. They live . . . the station.
9. He was standing . . . the fire.
10. Susan went to town . . . her mother.

G. *Put these sentences into the interrogative:*

1. Father Christmas brought them some presents.
2. There are some fish in that stream.
3. Tom went to Birmingham yesterday.
4. They drive to the seaside every Saturday.
5. She was playing cards with her friends.

6. David does his homework every evening.
7. He'll come home before six o'clock.
8. He can speak English very well.
9. His home is in London.
10. That book on the table is mine.

H. *Put the right word into these sentences:*

1. Mr Brown keeps his car in the . . .
2. A bicycle runs on two . . .
3. . . . comes between summer and winter.
4. When it is raining she carries an . . .
5. In the summer boys play . . ., in the winter they play . . .
6. In England, cars go on the . . . side of the road.
7. The first month of the year is . . ., the last month is . . .
8. We buy sugar at the . . . and cabbages at the . . .
9. We write with a . . . or a . . .
10. We eat meat with a . . . and . . .

I. *Write sentences beginning with these words (five sentences for each):*

How many . . . ?
How much . . . ?
How old . . . ?
How often . . . ?
At what time . . . ?

J. *Put the right verb into these sentences:*

1. Children are happy when Christmas . . .
2. I don't know where he is; I . . . him since last Thursday.
3. You . . . to bed if you are tired.
4. Susan and Tom . . . to London tomorrow, if it is fine.
5. Now you . . . your work, you can go home.
6. Mr Brown . . . in London, but he . . . in Bishopton.
7. Why was she carrying an umbrella? Because it . . .
8. He . . . his car into the garage and . . . the door.
9. Susan, . . . some flowers for your mother.
10. We . . . where he has gone.

K. *Write a composition about a city or town that you know well.*

L. *On page 150 there is a picture of a farmyard. Write ten sentences about this farmyard, and in each sentence use one of these prepositions:*

over; under; between; near; on; with; across; beside; into; round.

How Many?

A small boy was fishing by a stream. A man came by and stopped to watch him.

"How many have you caught?" the man asked.

"If I catch another, I shall have one," said the boy.

GRAMMAR SUMMARY 2

THE ENGLISH SENTENCE

The parts of a sentence are:

> The Subject   the Verb   the Object

The Subject and the Object are Nouns or Pronouns.

Subject	Verb	Object
The boy	*saw*	*his friend.*
The children	*are crossing*	*the street.*
I	*can play*	*football.*

Some verbs do not have an Object:

Birds	*sing.*
The boys	*were shouting.*
She	*is speaking.*

NOUNS

THE POSSESSIVE

For the Possessive of Nouns, add *'s*. If the Noun ends in *s*, add *'*. The Possessive Plural adds *'* because Plural Nouns usually end in *s*.

The *boy*'s book.	The *boy*'s books (one boy).
The *boys*' book.	The *boys*' books (more than one boy).
The *child*'s hand.	The *child*'s hands.
The *children*'s game.	The *children*'s games.
The *man*'s car.	The *man*'s cars.
The *men*'s car.	The *men*'s cars.

PRONOUNS

Pronouns stand for Nouns.

These are the Pronouns for the Subject; they are Subject Pronouns.

PERSONAL PRONOUNS

	Singular	Plural
The person speaking	*I*	*we*
The person he is speaking to	*you*	*you*
The person he is speaking about	*he, she, it*	*they*

These are the Pronouns for the Object: they are Object Pronouns.

Singular	Plural
me	*us*
you	*you*
him, her, it	*them*

I saw my friend.	My friend saw *me*.
You met your brother.	Your brother met *you*.
He took his sister to town.	His sister took *him* to town.
She saw her mother.	Her mother saw *her*.
We met our friends.	Our friends met *us*.
They left their friends.	Their friends left *them*.

POSSESSIVE ADJECTIVES AND PRONOUNS

Singular	Plural
my, mine	*our, ours*
your, yours	*your, yours*
his, his	
her, hers	*their, theirs*
its, its	

Adjectives	*Pronouns*
This is *my* book.	This book is *mine*.
That is *your* house.	That house is *yours*.
These are *his* friends.	These friends are *his*.

This is *her* car.	This car is *hers*.
This is *our* garden.	This garden is *ours*.
That is *their* picture.	That picture is *theirs*.

ADJECTIVES

COMPARISON OF ADJECTIVES

There are three forms for the Adjective in English:

(*a*) The first tells us about one person or thing:

> The boy is *tall*.

(*b*) The second compares one person or thing with one other:

> Of two boys, one is *taller* than the other.

(*c*) The third picks out one person or thing from many or all others:

> He is the *tallest* boy in the class.
> He is the *smallest* man in the world.

If the Adjective is a long word, we put *more* or *most* in front of it, instead of *-er* or *-est* after it:

> This is an *interesting* book.
> This book is *more interesting* than that.
> This is the *most interesting* book I have read.

Other Adjectives that take *more* and *most* are:

> *important, beautiful, expensive*.

SOME, ANY

In affirmative sentences (those that say 'yes') we use *some*; in negative sentences (those that say 'no') and in interrogative sentences (those that ask a question) we use *any*.

> She has *some* books.
> She hasn't *any* books.
> Has she *any* books?

VERBS

THE IMPERATIVE

This gives orders; it tells people to do something.
We use the Present Tense, without the pronoun *you*.

> (You) *Go* home, David.
> (You) *Come* here, Susan.
> *Cross* the road now, children.
> *Drive* slowly through the town.

Negative

Add *do not* (*don't*) to the Imperative.

> *Do not* (*don't*) *swim* in that cold water.
> *Do not* (*don't*) *get off* the bus until it stops.
> *Do not* (*don't*) *ask* any questions.

THE PAST CONTINUOUS TENSE

This Tense says what I *was doing* (a continuous action), and
not what I *did* (a single action).

The Past Tense of *Be* with the verb in *-ing* (the Present
Participle):

> I *was speaking*.
> He *was walking*.
> We *were swimming*.
> You *were running*.
> They *were eating*.

Negative

> I *was not* (*wasn't*) *speaking*.
> They *were not* (*weren't*) *eating*.

Questions

> *Was* I *speaking*?
> *Were* they *eating*?

THE PRESENT CONTINUOUS FOR THE FUTURE

We sometimes use the Present Continuous for the Future.

I *am going* to London tomorrow.
He *is coming* to see us next week.
He *is spending* his holidays in Switzerland next summer.
He *is taking* Susan to the theatre this evening.

WANT, LIKE, MUST, CAN, OUGHT

He *wants to go.*	He *must go.*
He *likes to go.*	He *can go.*
He *ought to go.*	

THE PRESENT PERFECT TENSE

In this tense we look at the past from the present, from *now*.

I *have finished* my work. (now)
I *have closed* the door. (It is closed now)
I *have put* the book on the table. (And it is there now)

We make the Present Perfect Tense with the Present Tense of *have* and the Past Participle.

Regular Verbs

The Past Participle usually adds *-ed*. It is the same as the Past Tense.

Present Tense	Past Tense	Past Participle
ask	*asked*	*asked*
cross	*crossed*	*crossed*
call	*called*	*called*
clean	*cleaned*	*cleaned*
enjoy	*enjoyed*	*enjoyed*
finish	*finished*	*finished*
help	*helped*	*helped*
jump	*jumped*	*jumped*
listen	*listened*	*listened*
look	*looked*	*looked*
open	*opened*	*opened*

play	played	played
pick	picked	picked
shout	shouted	shouted
start	started	started
*stop	stopped	stopped
*close	closed	closed
*change	changed	changed
*live	lived	lived
*like	liked	liked
*wave	waved	waved
*drop	dropped	dropped
*smoke	smoked	smoked
*carry	carried	carried
*hurry	hurried	hurried
*pay	paid	paid
*say	said	said
*try	tried	tried

*Notice these verbs.

Irregular Verbs

(a) The Past Participle the same as the Past Tense.

Present Tense	Past Tense	Past Participle
have	had	had
buy	bought	bought
dig	dug	dug
find	found	found
feed	fed	fed
get	got	got
hold	held	held
hear	heard	heard
leave	left	left
make	made	made
sit	sat	sat
stand	stood	stood
sell	sold	sold
shine	shone	shone
send	sent	sent

tell	told	told
think	thought	thought
put	put	put
cut	cut	cut
cost	cost	cost

Irregular Verbs

(b) The Past Participle different from the Past Tense.

Present Tense	Past Tense	Past Participle
begin	began	begun
go	went	gone
give	gave	given
grow	grew	grown
ring	rang	rung
sing	sang	sung
run	ran	run
swim	swam	swum
come	came	come
be	were	been
break	broke	broken
do	did	done
drive	drove	driven
eat	ate	eaten
fall	fell	fallen
speak	spoke	spoken
see	saw	seen
show	showed	shown
take	took	taken
tear	tore	torn
throw	threw	thrown
write	wrote	written
wear	wore	worn

THE THREE PAST TENSES

The *Past Tense*. Something that I did and finished in the past.
   I *went* to London last week.

The *Past Continuous Tense*. Something I was doing in the past.

I *was reading* a book when my friend came to see me.

The *Present Perfect Tense*. Something I have done in the past and it is finished now, but I am still thinking about it.

I *have written* a letter to my friend.

ADVERBS

We use adverbs with verbs. They tell *when, where, how, how much, how often* someone did something.

When: *yesterday, today, soon, now.*
Where: *here, there.*
How: *quickly, slowly, loudly, quietly, proudly, suddenly.*
How much: *nearly, almost.*
How often: *sometimes, often, always, once, twice, usually, ever, never.*

Adverbs which tell *how* often end in *-ly*.

The Place of the Adverb in the Sentence

1. In a sentence which has an object, we usually put the adverb after the object:

I met this man *yesterday*.

(*Never* put the adverb between the verb and the object):

2. In a sentence which hasn't an object, we usually put the adverb after the verb:

He was walking *slowly* down the street.

3. Adverbs which tell *how often* we usually put between the subject and the verb:

I *often* meet him in town.

Where the verb is in the Present Perfect tense, we usually put the *how often* adverb before the participle:

I have *usually* met him in London.
We have *often* visited Manchester.

Other adverbs like this are:

> *ever, never, almost, suddenly, sometimes, always, once, twice, nearly.*

PREPOSITIONS

A Preposition is a word which we put before a noun or pronoun to show the link between the noun or pronoun and another word in the sentence.

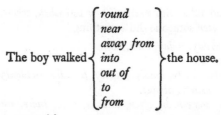

The boy walked { *round*, *near*, *away from*, *into*, *out of*, *to*, *from* } the house.

These are prepositions:

in	*into*	*before*
under	*through*	*behind*
on	*at*	*after*
near	*with*	*down*
to	*round*	*outside*
from	*off*	*inside*
up	*away from*	*beside*
by	*for*	*without*
between	*across*	*above*
	in front of	

After a Preposition we put an Object Pronoun, not a Subject Pronoun:

> I gave the book *to him.*
> We took the flowers *from her.*
> He was standing *near us.*
> We went to London *with them.*

These are Prepositional Phrases.

> *round the corner*   *in front of the house*

through the gate　　　*outside the station*
into the water　　　*down the street*
across the road

NEW WORDS

use, used (juːz, juːzd)
compare, compared (kəmˈpeə, kəmˈpeəd)

A Ride on a Tiger

There was a young lady of Riga,
Who went for a ride on a tiger;
　They came back from their ride
　With the lady inside,
And a smile on the face of the tiger.

lady (ˈleidi)
Riga (ˈraigə)
tiger (ˈtaigə)

LIST OF SENTENCE PATTERNS

(The numbers in brackets after the examples refer to pages.)

Grammatical Structure	Example
1. Present Tense of *Be*	*This is a table.* [14]
2. *What?*	*What is this?* [15]
3. Present Tense of *Be*	*He is a man.* [15]
4. Present Tense of *Be*— Questions	*Is this a man?* [15]
5. Present Tense of *Be*— Questions with short answers	*Is he a man? Yes, he is.* [16]
6. Present Tense of *Have*	*The man has a book.* [20]
7. Present Tense of *Have*— Questions	*Has he a book?* [21]
8. *Where?*	*Where is Mr Brown?* [21]
9. *What?* with Prepositional Phrases	*What have I in my hand?* [21]
10. Adjectives	*Susan is pretty.* [26]
11. Present Continuous Tense	*He is eating his breakfast.* [26]
12. Present Continuous— Negative	*He isn't eating his breakfast.* [27]
13. Present Continuous— Questions	*Is he eating his breakfast?* [27]
14. Possessive of Nouns	*This is Mr Brown's car.* [31]
15. Adjectives	*She is a pretty girl.* [32]
16. Sentence Structure— Subject, Verb, Object, Prepositional Phrase	*She is taking a letter from the postman.* [32]
17. *Who?*	*Who is in the car?* [32]
18. Past Tense of *Be*	*He was in London.* [37]
19. Past Tense of *Be*— Negative	*He wasn't in London.* [37]
20. Past Tense of *Be*— Questions	*Was he in London? Yes, he was.* [37]

LIST OF SENTENCE PATTERNS 233

	Grammatical Structure	Example
21.	Past Tense of *Have*	*He had a letter.* [38]
22.	Past Tense of *Have*—Negative	*He hadn't a letter.* [38]
23.	Simple Past Tense—Regular Verbs	*He walked to the station.* [44]
24.	Simple Past Tense—Irregular Verbs	*He went to London.* [45]
25.	Plurals—*A, Some*	*He has some matches.* [45]
26.	Simple Past Tense—Negative	*He didn't see the car.* [52]
27.	Simple Past Tense—Questions	*Did he see the car? Yes, he did. No, he didn't.* [53]
28.	Future Tense	*He will go to school tomorrow.* [59]
29.	Imperative	*Go to school, David.* [60]
30.	Imperative—Negative	*Don't take that book.* [60]
31.	Future Tense—Questions	*Will he go to school today?* [66]
32.	Future Tense—Negative	*He won't go to school today.* [67]
33.	Time—Hours	*It is one o'clock.* [67]
34.	Simple Present Tense	*He works in London.* [74]
35.	*How old?*	*How old is he? He is . . .* [75]
36.	Simple Present—Negative	*He doesn't go every day.* [82]
37.	Simple Present—Questions	*Does he go every day?* [82]
38.	*How much?*	*How much does it cost?* [83]
39.	Personal Pronouns	*I saw him. Give it to me.* [102]
40.	Possessive Adjectives	*He is eating his dinner.* [102]
41.	Time—the Quarter Hours	*It is a quarter past one.* [103]
42.	Verb and Infinitive	*He likes to go to school.* [112]
43.	Possessive Pronouns	*This book is mine.* [112]
44.	*There is, There are, There were*, etc.	*There is a book on the table.* [120]
45.	Impersonal *It*—Weather	*It is raining.* [120]
46.	*Some—Any*	*She has some chocolates. Has she any chocolates?* [128]
47.	Adverbs	*He is speaking quietly.* [128]
48.	Time—Minutes	*It is five past two.* [129]

Grammatical Structure	Example
69. *So*	*I think so. I hope so.* [204]
70. *Since*	*I have been here since Sunday.* [205]
71. Condition Clauses—*If*	*He will go home if he is ill.* [214]
72. Position of Frequency Adverbs	*He always plays football on Saturday.* [215]
73. Preposition at end of Sentence	*Who were you speaking to?* [215]
74. *Do*	*He is doing his homework.* [216]
75. *For*	*He has been here for a week.* [216]

INDEX TO THE EXERCISES

The numbers refer to the pages

WORD LIST

The numbers refer to the pages on which words first appear

a (ei, ə), 11
  an (an, ən), 43
about (ə'baut), 100
above (ə'bʌv), 126
across (ə'kros), 35
actor ('aktə), 127
  actress ('aktris), 127
add (ad), 89
afraid (ə'freid), 181
after ('aıftə), 73
afternoon ('aıftə'nuın), 58
again (ə'gen), 35
age (eidʒ), 143
ago (ə'gou), 120
air mail ('eə meil), 144
all (oıl), 51
along (ə'loŋ), 151
already (oıl'redi), 203
also ('oılsou), 117
always ('oılweiz, 'oılwəz), 73
am (see *be*) (am), 14
among (ə'mʌŋ), 80
and (and, ənd), 14
angry ('aŋgri), 51
animal ('animəl), 151
another (ə'nʌðə), 73
answer ('aınsə), 61
any ('eni), 126
  anything ('eniθiŋ), 145
apple ('apl), 79
April ('eiprl), 155

apron ('eiprən), 136
are (see *be*) (aı), 11
arm (aım), 51
  arm-chair ('aım 'tʃeə), 170
arrive (ə'raiv), 160
as (az, əz), 118
ask (aısk), 51
asleep (ə'sliıp), 73
at (at, ət), 26
August ('oıgəst), 153
aunt (aınt), 142
autumn ('oıtəm), 100
away (ə'wei), 50

baby ('beibi), 142
back (bak), 64
bacon ('beikən), 24
bag (bag), 19
baker ('beikə), 79
ball (boıl), 73
bank (baŋk), 50
basket ('baıskit), 153
be (biı)
  am (am, əm), 14
  are (aı), 11
  been (biın, bin), 176
  is (iz), 11
  was (woz, wəz), 35
  were (wəı, wə), 37
bean (biın), 79
beautiful ('bjuıtiful), 160

dug (dʌg)
dinner ('dinə), 64
   dining-room ('dainiŋ rum), 24
dirt (dəɪt), 137
   dirty ('dəɪti), 181
dish (diʃ), 137
do (duː), 26
   did (did)
   does (dʌz)
   done (dʌn)
dog (dog), 13
doll (dol), 212
door (doː), 11
down (daun), 35
dozen ('dʌzn), 81
dress (dres), 127
   noun, 127; *verb*, 151
drink (driŋk), 26
   drank (draŋk)
   drunk (drʌŋk)
   noun, 214
drive (draiv), 35
   drove (drouv)
   driven ('drivən)
   driver ('draivə), 51
drop (drop), 118
dry (drai), 80
during ('djuəriŋ), 212

each (iːtʃ), 81
early ('əːli), 110
east (iːst), 181
easy ('iːzi), 163
eat (iːt), 24
   ate (eit, et)
   eaten ('iːtn)

edge (edʒ), 181
egg (eg), 24
eight (eit), 67
   eighteen ('ei'tiːn), 151
electric (i'lektrik), 136
eleven (i'levn), 68
else (els), 203
empty ('emti), 65
end (end)
   noun, 89; *verb*, 99
enjoy (in'dʒoi), 127
enough (i'nʌf), 172
evening ('iːvniŋ), 64
ever ('evə), 215
every ('evri), 65
   everyone ('evriwʌn), 73
   everything ('evriθiŋ), 163
examination (ig'zami'neiʃn), 137
except (ik'sept), 72
excited (iks'aitid), 211
excuse (iks'kjuːz), 152
expensive (iks'pensiv), 126

face (feis), 52
factory ('faktəri), 109
fall (foːl), 50
   fell (fel)
   fallen (foːlən)
family ('famili), 135
far (faː), 73
fare (feə), 191
farm (faːm), 150
   farmer ('faːmə), 150
   farmhouse ('faːm'haus), 151
   farmyard ('faːmjaːd), 151

fast (faɪst), 36
fat (fat), 36
father ('faːðə), 25
favourite ('feivrit), 181
February ('februəri), 155
feed (fiːd), 151
   fed (fed)
few (fjuː), 145
field (fiːld), 100
fifteen ('fif'tiːn), 103
fifth (fifθ), 150
fifty ('fifti), 129
find (faind), 144
   found (faund)
fine (fain), 120
finish ('finiʃ), 78
fire ('faiə), 24
first (fəːst), 110
fish (fiʃ)
   verb, 73; noun, 181
five (faiv), 67
flask (flaːsk), 181
floor (floː), 118
flower ('flauə), 57
food (fuːd), 118
foot (fut), 36
   feet (fiːt)
football ('futbɔːl), 65
   footballer ('futbɔːlə), 100
for (fɔː, fə), 58
fork (fɔːk), 24
forty ('fɔːti), 129
forward ('fɔːwəd), 212
four (fɔː), 67
fourteen ('fɔː'tiːn), 119
fourth (fɔːθ), 152
fresh (freʃ), 80

Friday ('fraidi), 72
friend (frend), 35
   friendship ('frendʃip), 212
frighten ('fraitn), 162
from (from, frəm), 31
front (frʌnt), 126
fruit (fruːt), 66
full (ful), 101
funny ('fʌni), 127

gallery ('galəri), 126
game (geim), 66
garage ('garaːʒ, 'garidʒ), 35
garden ('gaːdn), 57
gas (gas), 136
gate (geit), 30
gay (gei), 126
gently ('dʒentli), 181
get (get), 42
   got (got)
girl (gəːl), 24
give (giv), 30
   gave (geiv)
   given ('givn)
glad (glad), 201
glass (glaːs), 65
glove (glʌv), 31
go (gou), 31
   went (went)
   gone (gon)
goal (goul), 190
gold (gould), 195
good (gud), 36
   better ('betə), 190
   best (best), 191
good-bye (gud'bai), 31
good-looking ('gud'lukiŋ), 65

in (in), 18
   inside ('in'said), 96
   into ('intu, intə), 30
instead (in'sted), 118
interesting ('intrəstiŋ), 162
invite (in'vait), 200
iron ('aiən), 136
is (see *be*) (iz), 11
it (it), 12
   its (its), 25

January ('dʒanjuəri), 153
jewel ('dʒuəl), 161
joy (dʒoi), 212
July (dʒu'lai), 153
jump (dʒʌmp), 151
June (dʒuːn), 150
just (dʒʌst), 152

keep (kiːp) 182
   kept (kept)
kettle ('ketl), 136
kindness ('kaindnis), 212
king (kiŋ), 162
kitchen ('kitʃin), 135
knife (naif), 24
knit (nit), 170
   knitting ('nitiŋ), 170
know (nou), 80
   knew (njuː)
   known (noun)

lady ('leidi), 231
large (laːdʒ), 43
last (laːst), 101
late (leit), 42
latest ('leitist), 201

laugh (laːf)
   verb, 126; *noun*, 127
learn (ləːn), 100
leave (liːv), 42
   left (left)
left (*noun* and *adjective*) (left),
   80
leg (leg), 182
lesson ('lesn), 100
let (let), 162
letter ('letə), 25
lettuce ('letis), 181
lift (lift), 144
light (lait), 125
like (laik), 73
listen ('lisn), 101
little ('litl), 25
live (liv), 72
loaf (louf), 80
long (loŋ), 160
look (luk), 110
lose (luːz), 182
   lost (lost)
lot (lot), 153
loudly ('laudli), 125
love (lʌv), 201
   lovely ('lʌvli), 150
luggage ('lʌgidʒ), 43
lunch (lʌntʃ), 58

machine (mə'ʃiːn), 143
madam ('madəm), 43
make (meik), 80
   made (meid)
man (man), 13
manager ('manidʒə), 50
many ('meni), 51

ought (oɪt), 202

our (see *we*) (auə), 19

ours (see *we*) (auəz), 112

out (aut), 50

  outside ('aut'said), 80

oven ('ʌvn), 136

over ('ouvə), 212

pack (pak), 180

packet ('pakit), 43

page (peidʒ), 172

paint (peint), 161

pantomime ('pantəmaim), 201

parliament ('paɪləmənt), 50

party ('paɪti), 200

pay (pei), 118

  paid (peid)

pear (peə), 66

pen (pen), 14

pencil ('pensl), 101

penny ('peni), 85

  pence (pens)

people ('piɪpl), 118

perhaps (pə'haps), 111

pick (pik), 111

picnic ('piknik), 180

picture ('piktʃə), 12

piece (piɪs), 100

pig (pig), 151

pillar-box ('piləboks), 36

pillow-case ('pilou keis), 211

place (pleis), 161

plate (pleit), 24

platform ('platfoɪm), 43

play (plei)

  verb, 65; *noun*, 125

player ('pleiə), 189

playing-field ('pleiiŋ fiɪld), 100

pleasant ('pleznt), 171

please (pliɪz), 31

  pleased (pliɪzd), 151

plenty ('plenti), 202

pocket ('pokit), 44

  pocket-knife ('pokitnaif), 117

point (point), 100

policeman (pə'liɪsmən), 35

polite (pə'lait), 80

porter ('poɪtə), 43

postal order ('poustəl oɪdə), 144

postman ('poustmən), 30

post office ('poustofis), 143

potato (pə'teitou), 79

pound (*money* and *weight*) (paund), 81

pour (poɪ), 118

present ('preznt), 200

pretty ('priti), 24

programme ('prougram), 126

proudly ('praudli), 182

pudding ('pudiŋ), 212

pull (pul), 182

put (put), 30

quarter ('kwoɪtə), 103

queen (kwiɪn), 160

question ('kwestʃn), 22

quickly ('kwikli), 58

quiet ('kwaiət), 125

  quietly ('kwaiətli), 127

radio ('reidiou), 171

noun, 73; *verb*, 79
  shopping ('ʃɔpiŋ), 79
short (ʃɔːt), 36
shoulder ('ʃouldə), 151
shout (ʃaut), 50
show (ʃou), 100
  shown (ʃoun)
side (said), 80
silly ('sili), 171
since (sins), 200
sing (siŋ), 151
  sang (saŋ)
  sung (sʌŋ)
single ('siŋgl), 43
sir (səː), 43
sister ('sistə), 24
sit (sit), 24
  sat (sat)
  sitting-room ('sitiŋrum), 18
six (siks), 64
sixteen ('siks'tiːn), 137
skirt (skəːt), 109
sky (skai), 73
sleep (sliːp), 202
  slept (slept)
slope (sloup), 181
slow (slou), 36
  slowly ('slouli), 125
small (smɔːl), 43
smart (smaːt), 117
smile (smail), 118
smoke (smouk), 74
so (sou), 50
soccer (Association football)
  ('sɔkə, ə'sousieiʃn
  'futbɔːl), 190
soldier ('souldʒə), 162

some (sʌm), 42
  someone ('sʌmwʌn), 152
  something ('sʌmθiŋ), 119
  sometimes ('sʌmtaimz), 72
son (sʌn), 24
soon (suːn), 59
sorry ('sɔri), 36
soup (suːp), 171
south (sauθ), 181
spade (speid), 136
speak (spiːk), 25
  spoke (spouk)
  spoken ('spoukən)
spend (spend), 143
  spent (spent)
spoon (spuːn), 24
spring (spriŋ), 100
stage (steidʒ), 126
stair (steə), 163
stall (stɔːl), 126
stamp (stamp), 143
stand (stand), 24
  stood (stud)
start (staːt), 66
station ('steiʃn), 31
stay (stei), 64
still (stil), 151
stocking ('stɔkiŋ), 211
stop (stop)
  verb, 35; *noun*, 191
story ('stɔːri), 124
stream (striːm), 181
street (striːt), 35
strike (straik), 160
  struck (strʌk)
strong (strɔŋ), 190
such (sʌtʃ), 212

tomato (təˈmaːtou), 181
tomorrow (təˈmorou), 59
tonight (təˈnait), 170
too (tuː), 51
tower (tauə), 160
town (taun), 58
toy (toi), 145
train (trein), 36
tray (trei), 74
tree (triː), 57
trousers (ˈtrauzəz), 100
try (trai), 101
  tried (traid)
Tuesday (ˈtjuːzdi), 72
turkey (ˈtəːki), 212
turn (təːn), 171
twelve (twelv), 68
twenty (ˈtwenti), 75
two (tuː), 67
type (taip), 109
  typewriter (ˈtaipraitə), 109

umbrella (ʌmˈbrelə), 43
under (ˈʌndə), 19
unhappy (ʌnˈhapi), 127
until (ənˈtil), 110
up (ʌp), 35
  upper (ˈʌpə), 126
us (see we) (ʌs), 102
use (juːz), 224
usually (ˈjuːʒuəli), 215

van (van), 80
vegetable (ˈvedʒ(i)təbl), 79
very (ˈveri), 36
visit (ˈvizit), 151
  visitor (ˈvizitə), 111

wait (weit), 111
  waitress (ˈweitris), 118
wake (weik), 150
  woke (wouk)
  woken (ˈwoukən)
walk (woːk), 35
wall (woːl), 11
want (wont), 80
warm (woːm), 31
  warmth (woːmθ), 212
was (see be) (woz, wəz), 35
wash (woʃ), 137
  washing-machine (ˈwoʃiŋ
    miʃiːn), 136
  washing-up (ˈwoʃiŋ ˈʌp), 214
watch (wotʃ)
  noun, 111; *verb*, 162
water (ˈwoːtə), 73
wave (weiv), 30
way (wei), 163
we (wiː), 19
  our (auə), 19
  ours (auəz), 112
  us (ʌs), 102
wear (weə), 109
  wore (woː)
  worn (woːn)
weather (ˈweðə), 120
Wednesday (ˈwenzdi), 72
week (wiːk), 100
well (wel), 36
were (see be) (wəː, wə), 37
west (west), 160
what (wot), 12
wheel (wiːl), 50
when (wen), 69
where (weə), 20

NAMES OF PLACES

BOYS' NAMES

Andrew (Andy) ('andruɪ, 'andi), 172
Anthony (Tony) ('antəni, 'touni), 200
Brian ('braɪən), 145
David ('deivid), 24
Frederick (Fred) ('fredrik, fred), 36
George (dʒɔːdʒ), 152
James (Jim) (dʒeimz, dʒim), 179

John (Jack) (dʒon, dʒak), 13
Joseph (Joe) ('dʒouzif, dʒou), 151
Patrick (Paddy) ('patrik, 'padi), 124
Robert (Bob) ('robət, bob), 180
Thomas (Tom) ('toməs, tom), 31
Toby ('toubi), 31

GIRLS' NAMES

Brenda ('brendə), 200
Ethel ('eθəl), 150
Joan (dʒoun), 81

Mary ('meəri), 13
Sheila ('ʃiːlə), 201
Susan ('suːzn), 24

FAMILY NAMES

Barnes (baɪnz), 101
Brook (bruk), 35
Brown (braun), 13
Campbell ('kambl), 137
Johnson ('dʒonsn), 172
Jones (dʒounz), 80
Mason ('meisn), 200
Morton ('moɪtn), 79

Randall ('randl), 111
Robinson ('robinsn), 100
Sandford ('sanfəd), 180
Smith (smiθ), 31
Stansbury ('stanzbri), 151
Stephens ('stiɪvnz), 80
Stone (stoun), 179
Thompson ('tomsn), 100

GRAMMATICAL TERMS

action ('akʃn)
adjective ('adʒiktiv)
adverb ('advəːb)
affirmative (ə'fəːmətiv)
clause (kloːz)
comparison (kəm'parisən)
composition ('kompəziʃn)
condition (kən'diʃn)
consonant ('konsənant)
continuous (kən'tinjuəs)
conversation ('konvə'seiʃn)
dictation (dik'teiʃn)
exercise ('eksəsaiz)
frequency ('friːkwənsi)
future ('fjuːtʃə)
grammar ('gramə)
idiom ('idiəm)
imperative (im'perətiv)
impersonal (im'pəːsənl)
infinitive (in'finitiv)
interrogative (intə'rogativ)
irregular (i'regjulə)
link (liŋk)
list (list)
negative ('negətiv)
noun (naun)
object ('obdʒikt)
order ('oːdə)
part (paːt)

participle ('paːtisipl)
past (paːst)
pattern ('patən)
perfect ('pəːfikt)
person ('pəːsn)
personal ('pəːsnəl)
phrase (freiz)
plural ('pluːrəl)
position (pə'ziʃn)
positive ('pozitiv)
possessive (pə'zesiv)
preposition ('prepə'ziʃn)
present ('prezənt)
pronoun ('prounaun)
quality ('kwoliti)
question-tag ('kwestʃn 'tag)
reading ('riːdiŋ)
reason ('riːzn)
regular ('regjulə)
relative ('relətiv)
sentence ('sentəns)
simple ('simpl)
singular ('siŋgjulə)
subject ('sʌbdʒikt)
summary ('sʌməri)
tense (tens)
verb (vəːb)
vowel ('vauəl)
word (wəːd)